If the Church
Is to Survive . . .

A best-selling Catholic author of the last decade here summarizes the conditions which, in his opinion, must be met if the Church is to continue to exist. He calls for a Church that conforms both to the Gospel and to the needs of the time: "a democratic Church in which all authority will rest with the People of God, and in which the People of God will have every ministry at its disposal."

Evely feels that consolation therapy has had its day, and that it is now time for shock therapy. To some, his suggestions for reform will be radical and controversial. But few can deny that there is indeed a crisis in the Church and confusion among the faithful. The crisis is not, as Evely makes clear, a crisis of faith as such, but rather a crisis of confidence in the hierarchy and the hierarchical system.

(continued on back flap)

(continued from front flap)

Separate chapters examine such critical areas as authority, the institutional and structural church, and the religious life. A concluding section offers a general commentary on the "Church in the Service of the World." In this last section, the author calls for the Church to abandon its traditional spiritual imperialism and become truly *universal* in its ambitions.

If the Church
Is to Survive . . .

by

Louis Evely

translated by

J. F. Bernard

Doubleday & Company, Inc.
Garden City, New York, 1972

Originally published in France under the title:
Si l'église ne meurt . . .
© Editions Universitaires, 1971

ISBN: 0-385-03846-1
Library of Congress Catalog Card Number 72–79374
Translation Copyright © 1972 by Doubleday & Company, Inc.
All Rights Reserved
Printed in the United States of America
First Edition

1709327

Contents

Christ summons the Church, as she goes her pilgrim way, to that continual reformation of which she always has need, insofar as she is an institution of men here on earth.

(Decree on Ecumenism, 6)

How to Use This Book

MY PURPOSE IN WRITING THIS BOOK IS TO DESCRIBE THE CONDITIONS BY WHICH THE Church will be able to fulfill its necessary mission of preaching the Gospel and inspiring faith.

No one can pretend to foresee the face that the Church will present, or must present, to the world in the next few years. And yet, everyone imagines what it will be like, and, consciously or not, contributes to its formation. This book is an exercise in that kind of imaginative effort. It is not intended to be, like its predecessors, merely a stimulus to reflection and an invitation to reaction. It is certainly open to criticism; and, indeed, it invites criticism to define its ideas.

Everyone recognizes the necessity of reforming the structures of the Church, of arriving at a new understanding and a new formulation of the faith, of developing a way of preaching the Gospel that is in keeping with the needs of our contemporaries. One wonders how many more books like this one will be needed—books which discuss these problems without even pretending to arrive at solutions.

I have been (and still am) accused of a harsh and aggressive style. Well, Bernanos used to say that "irony is a groaning of the soul." I love the Church too much not to suffer over its deformations, not to become indignant over them. We have too much need of the Church, of that community in which others help us to live beyond our own abilities, for us not to protest against anything that drives away, or alienates, men of good will. I am, I admit, hard on the Church. But the Church is all of us; and have I not the right to be hard on myself? To be impatient with anything in the Church that abases, dehumanizes, and discourages so many people? What I criticize, sometimes in strong terms, is the same thing that I once believed so strongly (and so wrongly), and that I taught to those who came to me for guidance. The violence of my attacks, therefore, may be understandable in the light of how difficult and painful it is to rid oneself of such beliefs.

For some people, every criticism of the Church is a sort of treason, an offense, an act of destruction. Yet only a society that is feeble and archaic cannot abide criticism.

Vatican II taught us that many of the things we used to accept as truths of the faith are not quite so; or that they are merely the opinions of theologians. As one Catholic review put it: "We have been able to establish a list of twenty-eight points which, yesterday, were sustained by Protestants and were regarded as heretical, and which are today defended by Catholic theologians."[1] We now know, in the wake of the Council, that many of the laws that we used to observe—and that we unfortunately compelled others to observe—under pain of mortal sin, were actually matters of little importance. We now admit that the Protestants were correct in using a living language for their services, in emphasizing the priesthood of the faithful, the primacy of the Scripture, the inspiration which makes a prophet of every Christian,

---

[1] *Informations Catholiques Internationales*, No. 347, p. 9.

the participation of the laity, and the rights of conscience. Let us not wait for Vatican III to continue revising our ideas. If we do, then we will have to resign ourselves to lagging behind our nonbelieving contemporaries, or simply behind those who are younger than we.

The way in which I talk about the Church offends some people. But then, everyone has his own way of doing things. And, for that matter, no one is forced to read what I write. It is possible to scandalize the weak; but it is also possible to scandalize the strong—a scandal of which the Church herself has been guilty on more than one occasion. In my opinion, there are more than enough genteel books—works that speak very softly and upset no one—to satisfy the whole world. Consolation therapy has had its day. It is now time for shock therapy.

The present crisis of the Church consists in its division between two irreconcilable groups: the "old ones," who cannot, or will not, admit liturgical, disciplinary, and conceptual changes; and the young ones, who are repelled by the old ceremonies, beliefs, and practices. It is impossible to speak to both groups at once. Every priest today finds that his parish is really two parishes. What awakens faith, or at least stirs interest among young people, scandalizes their elders to the point that they lose what little faith they have left. And to lead older people from the traditional faith to one that is more personal requires so much time, so much patience, and so many precautions that the young people have not the patience to listen to, let alone to read, anything about it. (They read so little of anything, for that matter.)

If we want to preserve the faith for new generations,

we must speak to them in a language that is understandable. We must not confuse beliefs with faith. What is essential in faith is not a catalog of dogmas, but the perception of the spiritual reality of Christ; actual contact with Christ; an experience of Christ's life-giving power in his Word, in his forgiveness, in his love.

What surprises me most about criticisms of my books is that many bishops, priests, and laymen have read them, or at least leafed through them, without ever seeming to notice the apostolic fervor, the living faith, the spiritual experience, that was obvious to so many others. They seemed content to note only the discrepancies between what I said and what they believed, without ever becoming aware of the underlying faith that is common to us all.

I have been accused, on the one hand, of attempting to destroy the faith; and, on the other, of beating dead horses. My intention, however, has been merely to draw both "new things and old things" from the treasury of Scripture. If I only repeat what has been said before me, then what good is it for me to write? And if the ideas I express are taken whole and entire from my own mind, what a high opinion I must have of myself. But if I am able to lead one to a new and living reading of the Gospel and a new understanding of the situation of the Church, then I will have rendered the service that I set out to do.

*   *   *

I had at first intended to entitle this section *Introduction: How to Use Evely Properly;* or, *Please Do Not Get Excited Until You Have Read the Book.* But, remembering the general indignation that once greeted an unfortunate reference by me to "my promotion to the lay state," I hesitate to rely upon the sense of humor of Catholics. I have been accused of attempting to humiliate my former confreres, and of priding myself upon my fall from the clerical state. I should be horrified, I suppose. Instead, I have to smile. The term, "reduction to the lay state" obviously contains an element offensive to the faithful; and also something comical in it that is vaguely evocative of head-hunting along the Amazon. If the ministers of the Church are truly the servants of the laity, then which is the superior, and which the inferior? There is a parable about those who chose the last place so that they may be invited to take first place . . .

The truth of the matter is that I asked to be "reduced to the lay state," not in order to leave the Church, but to be rid of a title that branded me as a representative of the hierarchy. It seemed to me hypocritical to continue to appear to represent that group when I was no longer in agreement with it. For my part, these differences with the hierarchy seemed secondary and temporary; but, to the authorities, they seemed primary and essential. There is no such thing as a conscientious objector in the Church. A priest who "contests the exercise of authority in the Church, even though he does not reject it in principle," according to the Declaration of the Permanent Committee of French Bishops, has no alternative but to go.

In conferences and retreats, I always used to warn my listeners that what I was offering were my own personal opinions. "Never," I warned them, "believe a priest. A priest is only a part of the Church teaching.

He is not *the* Church teaching. Whoever believes every-thing that one priest says will inevitably find another priest who says exactly the opposite." I used to tell them that they must learn to think for themselves, basing them-selves on what they had learned from all sources. They laughed; but they continued nonetheless to give more credence to what I said because I was a priest—that is, a representative of the hierarchy—than because of any inherent truth that they saw in my words.

Now, that situation no longer exists. Whoever reads this book must regard it as the participation of a lay Christian in his Church's effort at renewal.

A more serious objection is this: "Why speak of the Church? No one is interested in the Church any more. We are tired of her superficial reforms; irritated by her continued resistance on questions that have already been settled, such as social justice and priestly celibacy; shocked by her total helplessness in the battle for justice and for human freedom."

The young people say, "Speak to us about ourselves, about the world, about the future. Speak to us even about Jesus Christ and the Gospel. But leave the dead to bury their dead. What you say about faith, about human brotherhood, about collective hope, interests us. But you will never make us believe that we will make any progress in those things by going to church."

Yet, I remain convinced that a true Church is indis-pensable to the world. The Gospel is not an ideology, but a life. It must be passed on by living men, by little groups sufficiently united in brotherhood for brother-hood to be communicated among them. If the day comes that the Gospel is nothing more than a book in a library, then the Gospel will be as dead as those religions to which we are not bound by unbroken tradition. The true Church is a community in which the Gospel of Jesus is lived. The faith is dying because so few of our contemporaries have ever gone beyond the Church-building and the Church-administering to the Church in which Christ is alive through the assembly of his members.

But how can the Church—that is, all of us who, willing or not, have been influenced by her—place herself at the service of the world if she does not undergo a profound reformation? How can Christians create a revolution outside the Church if they refuse to create one within the Church? How can the Church take up the battle on behalf of the poor and the oppressed if the Pope remains a chief of state bound to other chiefs of state not only by diplomatic relations, but also by a common mentality and common interests? The new revolution is supposed to create a world characterized by freedom and brotherhood; but Christians cannot participate in such a revolution with all their hearts so long as they hold on to the idea of a sovereign, self-sufficient, and omnipotent God, and of an authoritarian, wealthy, and unchanging Church, both of which bless the old relationships of domination and class. If we are to revolutionize human relations, we must, like Jesus Christ, revolutionize religious relations.

Chapter One

The Present Crisis

> *"It is possible to admire the Catholic Church without being a Catholic. And perhaps it is also possible to be a Catholic without admiring the Catholic Church."*
>
> —Hans Küng, in *The Church*

THE CRISIS IN THE CHURCH GROWS WORSE DAY BY DAY.
There is confusion among the faithful, who do not know whether their faith should be used to conserve as much as possible of the past, as their old pastors taught them, or to promote the attempts at renewal that are proposed to them by their new pastors.

There is confusion among the leaders of the Church, who feel that they are no longer listened to, who see their authority challenged (and violently challenged) both by those who think that they are going too far and by those who think they are not going far enough. And they see their orders and exhortations received with general indifference.

There is latent schism between two groups of Catholics who cannot abide each other and who have broken off the fraternal dialogue between themselves that they claim to be carrying on with outsiders.

There has been a failure of remedies now perceived as tragically disproportionate to the cases they were supposed to cure—in the case of the Council, for instance, which compromised between the timid majority and the powerful minority. And, since that time, the Curia has never ceased attempting to slow down the application of the Council's decrees, while awakened Christians are no longer struggling to implement those decrees because they regard them as already outdated, and they are looking forward to Vatican III.

This crisis will not be resolved by time. The time that

is being gained by the Church is being lost by men. Instead, this crisis will engender new and bigger crises. We must remember that life is crisis, and where there is no crisis there is no life. What is disturbing about all this is the amount of time, of clumsiness, that is involved in the Church's evolution; it is the virtual inability of the Church's organism to react; it is the mixture of paralysis and agitation that afflicts the Church. The true solution is not to suppress crises, but for the Church to find the flexibility, the vitality, and the cohesion that are necessary for her to resolve those crises.

Merely to denounce the depth and extent of evil will scandalize only those who have too little faith and too little strength to fight evil in the first place. Such men are, unfortunately, particularly numerous among traditional Catholics, who have been trained to regard their "pastors" with blind and passive trust. What we need now are men and women who are open, intelligent, honest, and free, who have put aside a Church in which they could no longer breathe, and who have many of the qualities that are necessary to reformation.

There is always the risk that, in asking too much, we will find ourselves left with nothing. But, the Catholic Church is nothing if not the property of the whole of humanity, and the disappearance of her influence is a possibility that affects everyone. Above all, we must remember that the Gospel can survive only if it is transmitted and lived within a Church.

Let us therefore attempt to diagnose what ails us, and probe our wounds to discover what has caused them to become infected. Let us recall that the age of an organism can be determined by the amount of time that is required for its wounds to heal, and by its inability to adapt and transform itself. The Church has survived many crises. Her powerlessness before the present crisis obviously has nothing to do with her evangelical message, which is always young and ever new, nor with a lack of contact with the Spirit, which, to the contrary, now moves over us almost violently. The problem is rather that the Church has become a prisoner of her own traditions and structures rather than of the Gospel; and she is therefore left open to Christ's reproach: "You replace the Word of God by your own traditions, which have been handed down by yourselves" (Mark 7:13).

*   *   *

Ecclesiastical authority, ironically enough, has not been discredited in the eyes of Catholics by its abuses or its errors, but by its reforms. So great is the passivity and credulity of men, and particularly of pious men, that, if the system had continued to declare itself infallible and sacred, it would have retained much more of its old credibility and authority than it has in trying to reform itself. This is the phenomenon of "de-Stalinization." As soon as one begins to pick away at an idol's clay feet, there is no way to keep it from toppling over. The only ones who will be surprised by this fact are those who are unaware that excessive submission is a cover for revolt; that aggressiveness is a mask of fear; and that adherence to routine is laziness in disguise.

We have been reared in a religion of fear. The Church seemed to multiply, arbitrarily, the number of mortal sins, the reasons for excommunication and damnation.

One could be consigned to an eternity of hellfire for swallowing a drop of water before receiving the Eucharist, for eating an ounce of meat on Friday, for doing a bit of work on Sunday, for missing Mass on a day of obligation, for not confessing a mortal sin, for reading a book on the Index, for engaging in marital relations without allowing a child to be conceived.

In retrospect, all this seems unbelievable. But the most unbelievable thing of all is that we believed it with all our hearts. And, as we picked our way gingerly through the maze of ecclesiastical regulations, not daring to stray a hair's breadth to the right or left, we swallowed almost without noticing it the monstrous facts of social injustice, of division among Christians, of war, of the political and economic colonization of the Third World.

Strangely enough, this religion of ours was able to reassure us by its very severity. Within the Church, everything was certain, everything was sacred; and within her there was a safe haven for those who were disturbed by the rapidity of change in the world and by new ideas.

To be Catholic meant to be a reactionary in the modern world, to be a brake on progress, to be a fugitive from history. There are many people alive today who remember when to be a "good Catholic" meant to be for Franco in the Spanish war, to be for Mussolini in the Ethiopian and Albanian wars, to be for Salazar in Portugal. The only thing that saved a Catholic from being a pro-Nazi (despite the temptation to admire those proponents of law and order who had signed a Concordat with the Pope) was a patriotic reflex, combined with the possibility of becoming one of the victims of those same Nazis.

For two centuries, "good Catholics" were supposed to be opposed to democracy, freedom of the press, freedom of discussion, and freedom of opinions. They were supposed to be against tolerance, socialism, atheistic science, evolution, psychiatry, equal rights, mandatory education, emancipation of the female, sexual education, birth control, and ecumenism.

On the other hand, they were supposed to defend the temporal power of the Pope; and three hundred bishops, on the eve of Vatican I, signed a declaration to the effect that the States of the Church were indispensable to the exercise of the Pope's spiritual power.

Faith had become a discipline. A Catholic was not supposed to try to understand. He was required only to adhere to formulas and adopt a certain line of conduct. The reading of the Bible itself was forbidden (under pain of mortal sin, naturally), so there remained only one source of faith: the magisterium of the Church, which was exercised without control.

Anything new was tantamount to infidelity. To speak of the Holy Spirit, of the gift of prophecy, of the priesthood of the faithful, of a "religious experience," was to leave oneself open to a charge of heresy. Catholics were not expected to live their faith, only to preserve it and transmit it intact. The surest way to do this, of course, was not to inspect it too closely. "Good Catholics" were not supposed to think. They were supposed to rely upon their pastors to dictate to them the faith that they professed.

To believe in the Church in those days meant that one was dispensed from knowing God, for to listen to one's pastor was the same as listening to God. Faith was a social virtue, and eternal salvation was assured by docility and submission to the Church—even if one had never personally experienced Jesus Christ.

Cardinal Daniélou was still writing in 1968: "For a Christian, faith essentially consists in having confidence in another person about those things that one has not experienced oneself, but that the other has experienced. . . . The very concept of faith is to rely totally upon the witness of another."[1]

The Christian, in other words, is not supposed to try to find out what God wants of him. He is supposed to rely upon the Church to tell him. To be Christian, therefore, means not only to abdicate one's critical intelligence but also one's own religious experience, and to renounce any inspiration from the Holy Spirit.[2]

For most believers, the Credo was merely an abstruse formula. One could assure oneself of salvation by reciting it; but the only really practical thing in it was the phrase about the forgiveness of sins.

The Church had become a vast body, the entire weight of which rested upon its head. And the more the vitality of Christians ebbed, the more the power of the hierarchy was rendered absolute. There were no longer any limits

[1] *Liberté et autorité dans l'Eglise,* pp. 11–13. And "another" is obviously the Church (i.e., the hierarchy) to which Christ transferred his competence (p. 12).
[2] Here is a significant passage from St. Ignatius' *Spiritual Exercises,* the Thirteenth Rule of Orthodoxy: "To be just in all things, I must be prepared, when I see something that is white, to believe that it is black if the hierarchy of the Church decides that it is so."

to credulity. Superstition flourished, and the faithful were eager for the most transparent apparitions and the most infantile "messages." And why not? They had been taught to regard everything as a "truth of faith"—miracles, angels, demons, the continuing virginity of Mary after the birth of Jesus, the existence of Adam and Eve, the preternatural gifts of Adam (he was exempt from suffering, ignorance, concupiscence, and death), an earthly paradise, the infallibility of canonizations (even though a few of them had to be retracted from time to time), the beatific vision of Jesus and the perfection of knowledge in him from the first moment of his conception—the list is endless.

The comparatively recent dogmas of the Immaculate Conception, the Assumption, the infallibility of the Pope, awakened no criticism to speak of. In fact, the faithful would have swallowed things even more marvelous than these if they had been told to do so. Today, however, we have been awakened. We may ask ourselves what the "Immaculate Conception" means, when we no longer know what original sin is (the myth of collective responsibility without personal participation!). We wonder what we mean by the "Assumption," since we no longer believe in the literal resurrection of the body. We are puzzled by infallibilty in an age when the Church admits her errors, her faults, and her failings.

Christ intended the Church to be a source of truth, a means for liberating and educating the human conscience, and as such was to be distinguished from the oppressiveness of the law. Instead, it has become, in the opinion of many, an instrument of enslavement in the style of a totalitarian dictatorship. It has replaced the spirit with the law, charisma with commandments, and inspiration with obligation.

For centuries, the Church has exercised and re-inforced its authority in a manner reminiscent more of the Roman Empire than of an institution founded by a Christ who was poor, gentle, and humble of heart.

When we consider the bondage in which, for so many hundreds of years, it has held its priests, its monks, and especially its nuns, and when we see the political, social, religious, and economic conditions of the countries in which the Church is dominant, then we wonder what message of freedom it is able to proclaim to the world. We wonder, too, what would remain of our rights if we were not protected by secular states against this Church which claims to be inspired by the freedom of the Spirit.

*   *   *

Nonetheless, despite evidence of these errors, these misuses of authority, these betrayals of the evangelical ideal, Catholics remained obedient and trusting. It was not until the Council, when the Church began to question herself, to admit her sins, to change her laws, to re-articulate her doctrines, that the faithful, now disenchanted, began to awaken to their responsibilities.

Many people are nostalgic for their former state of slavery. They remember with longing the security and the prestige of that closed, rigid, unchanging universe of Catholicism. They exhibit a hostility toward the self-reforming Church that is more virulent than that of progressives who regard the whole process of reformation as impossibly slow. It would be amusing, if it were not

so sad, to see these partisans of blind submission re-
volting against authority when that authority bids them
do something other than what they have always done.

This sort of hostility or surliness is one of the most
distressing characteristics of the present-day Church, and
one of the most paradoxical in a day of ecumenical
sentiment. Catholics are now open to dialogue with non-
Christian religions and even with atheists; but they are
closed to mutual understanding and respect in their
own Church.

This curious phenomenon may be explained by the
confusion of men who have not been educated to, and
are therefore not accustomed to, freedom of thought and
the distinction between what is essential and what is
accidental. They were always taught that they had to
accept everything—or nothing. It is not surprising that
they still belong to the all-or-nothing school. The interior
struggle to bring themselves to accept submission now
makes them inflexibly opposed to those who regard as
unimportant what they themselves were taught to accept
as sacred. And they look upon progressives as icono-
clasts, or heretics, or schismatics.

Look at the Church in Holland, full of common sense,
of vitality and freedom; a unique example of cohesion
between the clergy and the faithful. Yet traditional
Christians suspect the Dutch Church *en masse* of schism.
They isolate her, accuse her, refuse to discuss or consult
with her, reject the experiments that she proposes, and
misunderstand the legitimate autonomy of her local
churches.

Such is the attitude of the Church toward those enclaves of life and renewal, those informal and ever more numerous groups upon which the future of Catholicism depends.

Catholics must learn to live in a pluralistic society, to recognize as faithful to the Gospel even those who interpret the Gospel differently, and who make a different application of the Gospel message to their lives. If not, the Church will end up consisting only of those who refuse to be disturbed in their habit of belief; a habit that has gradually changed into one of non-belief. It will consist of those who hope only that nothing will change; and who love only those who resemble themselves. And, at that point, the Church will have become an anachronistic sect. Even now, the Church is being deserted by the educated classes as rapidly as she was by the working classes in the nineteenth century.

*   *   *

We must stop the terrible and silent exodus of those who leave the Church because they are discouraged. Above all, we must find a way to put an end to the endemic indifference to authority which exists among those who remain.

In Europe, in the German-occupied countries, we were taught by World War II to disregard established authority and to ignore bishops who collaborated with the Nazis. Everyone believed that this "crisis of authority" would disappear when the exceptional circumstances that produced it had also disappeared. Instead, we find that this attitude, instead of disappearing, has become generalized. Vatican II, by consecrating what the hierarchy had so long condemned, has taught many Catholics that one can serve the Church by engaging in a limited battle against her. And they continue the fight by preparing for Vatican III.

The French experience of Catholic Action, of labor unions, of the student uprising of May 1968, of political and international commitment, has made people lose faith in ecclesiastical directives. They know that whatever they have learned or done of value in those circumstances has been without, or even in spite of, their religious leaders, and in reaction against what they were taught from their earliest years. They know that authority long attempted to throw them off the track, to put off as long as possible the moment when they would recognize truths that they had always felt existed and that atheists had known for a long time. They know that unbelievers have sometimes been more useful than theologians in rediscovering the Gospel, and that, when they were aided by priests or militant laymen, these men were always on the fringes of the Church and suspect in her eyes. And this is what they concluded from this evidence: that, for the last three centuries, it seems that the Holy Spirit has breathed more often outside the Church, on the humanists and philosophers, the socialists and scientists, than within the Church.

It is worth noting that this crisis of faith in the hierarchy is generally accompanied by a revival of enthusiasm for the Gospel. And this points out the way to salvation for us. If the hierarchy of its own accord once more becomes evangelical, it will abandon its pretentions to infallibility, prestige, and omnipotence. It will admit that its existence can be justified only on the basis of the service that it renders. It is true that, in conscience, one is bound to listen and obey in the presence of a true spiritual authority. But a spiritual police state can elicit only revolt.

Chapter Two

Authority in the Church[1]

"Authority" killed Christ.
But Christ has destroyed authority.

[1] This chapter has been largely and broadly inspired by Hans Küng's excellent book *The Church*. It does not, however, follow his thinking in all respects—and this acknowledgment of indebtedness should not be construed as an attempt to saddle Küng with the blame for my own ideas.

HERBERT MCCABE, THE ENGLISH DOMINICAN WHO WAS DI-
RECTOR OF THE *New Blackfriars* review, wrote the following sentence to explain the departure of Charles Davis
from the Church: "The Church is obviously corrupt." For
that offense, McCabe was suspended from his priestly
functions; and, three years later, he was reinstated. This
represents progress. Before Vatican II, McCabe would
never have been reinstated; or, if he had been, it would
have been done posthumously.

The corruption of which McCabe wrote has to do
above all with the use of ecclesiastical power, and it
follows the old adage: "Power corrupts, and absolute
power corrupts absolutely." One would have to look a
long time to find a power more absolute than that tra-
ditionally claimed by the Catholic Church.

Any discussion of authority in the Church must begin
with a definition of authority according to the Gospel.
After that, it will be easy—indeed, almost unnecessary—
to describe and explain the abuses of authority from
which the Church suffers.

The Holy Spirit: Sole Authority in the Church

"Even more than secular power, power
in the Church may seem to be the only
means for doing good. It is not always
easy to see that, when we put our faith

in power, we are actually giving up our
faith in the Spirit."

—John McKenzie,
Authority in the Church

The only authority in the Church is the Spirit of Jesus, the
Spirit that no one can monopolize, control, or manipulate.
The Spirit moves where, when, and in the manner that it
wishes. The only limitation of the Spirit consists in human freedom, for the Spirit of God is a spirit of freedom.
It can only *offer* itself to man; for man once deprived of
liberty is no longer man. The Spirit gives of itself "without reserve", for Jesus pours out his spirit "on all mankind" (John 3:34; and Acts 2:17). If it is true, therefore,
that the Spirit has made its home in the Church, it is
also true that it has innumerable secondary domiciles.

Even the government of the Church is a gift of the
Spirit, a "charisma"—that is, an aptitude for receiving
and communicating inspiration.[2]

The crisis of every society consists in the division of
that society between its institutions and its inspiration—
a division that results in the proliferation of institutions
and the concomitant decrease in inspirations. Through-
out the history of the Church, its leaders have attempted

---

[2] We can distinguish between:
  (a) *Charisma*, which is a gift of the Spirit (a vocation, a call) and
      which makes a man capable of rendering a special service
      within the community. The supreme charisma is love, but there
      are many others. Every man has his own charisma, for we are
      all animated by the Spirit. It may be a natural gift, but
      qualified by a call to service in the community.
  (b) *The ministry*, which is the service of government conferred by
      the imposition of hands (ordination). It is a charisma like the
      others, but a charisma institutionalized by a rite.

to create an organism strong enough, in human terms, to be able to do without the Holy Spirit. Administration stifled life, and the faithful were transformed into "subjects"—if not into objects. Every precaution was taken for this organism to be able to function ideally without the occurrence of the unexpected, without prophets, without heaven-sent apostles like Paul, without participation by the people in government, without any manifestation of the Holy Spirit outside the established chain of command.

The Church became more and more divine; and the Spirit was spoken of less and less. It was forgotten that the Christian, and even the Catholic, does not believe in the Church, for the Church is the People of God, it is all of us. And we do not believe in ourselves. We put our faith in the Holy Spirit who acts within the Church when the Church is humble and attentive. The true meaning of the Credo is this: "I believe in the Holy Spirit in the Catholic Church. . . ."

This, no doubt, is the reason why, for the past three centuries, the Spirit seems to have found a more attentive audience, and a more fruitful one, among the pagans and the atheists, in the world of sociologists, scientists, and artists, than in the Church. The Church's attention has been occupied with herself and her past, while the Spirit is the spirit of creation and openness. It cannot be imprisoned within a formula or a temple, for its nature is to spread over the whole world. If the dove of the Holy Spirit were allowed to light only on Catholics, it would have to remain in flight for a very long time. Happily, the

Spirit of the Lord fills the whole universe, and it moves where it will.

Nonetheless, there is no intrinsic opposition between institution and inspiration. On the contrary, although an institution without inspiration is intolerable, it must be said that true inspiration tends to create an institution. True love creates marriage. A genius creates a work, and often a school. True faith creates a Church.

What we must understand is that, if the Church wishes to remain under the guidance of the Spirit, the pastoral ministry must be considered as a charisma—so much so that a minister without charisma cannot be a true minister. It is useless to try to govern unless one has the "gift" of governing. There are, of course, false prophets, those who have not the "gift of prophecy." But there are also false pastors, who lack the ability to lead. One can abuse a charisma; but the worst abuse is to attempt to operate without one. It is said that the freedom accompanying such charismas threatens the good order of the Church. But Küng replies: "Was it really worse for a community as notoriously alive as that at Corinth to have disorder in its worship, than for a community to fall into that fatal indifference and disinterest into which worship led by established ministers has so often, and so quickly, led?"[3] Christian communities—"grass-roots communities" —have existed[4] and exist at present without hierarchically

[3] Hans Küng, *The Church* (New York, Sheed & Ward, 1967), p. 583.
[4] *Ibid.* ". . . At Corinth, for example, there were neither bishops nor priests, nor any ordinations of any sort, but, with the exception of the Apostle, charismas sprang up spontaneously. In spite of that, the Church of Corinth, a community lacking every necessity, was fortified by the preaching of the Word, by Baptism, by the Last Eucharist and by all the services." Küng, pp. 607–8.

appointed or ordained ministers; while many traditional communities are being smothered by the devotion to routine, the authoritarianism and the intolerance of their sacralized pastors.

The obvious application of this is to choose ministers not from among the docile bureaucrats but from among the charismatics. There are many perfectly authentic charismas that are not sanctioned by a hierarchical structure; but there should not be a hierarchical structure without charisma.

For centuries, the Church has acted as though charismas were at the beck and call of authority and as though once a charisma was received, it endured forever. Vocations were planted and cultivated in novitiates and in minor seminaries. But would it not have been more sensible and more respectful of the freedom of the Spirit first to allow the charisma to show itself to those most concerned; that is, to the consumers? And would it not have been more prudent to provide periodic tests to make sure that a charisma, once received, was still present? It is paradoxical to observe how, in this respect, civil service is conceived along more evangelical lines than is religious service. The problem is that the Church has held on to the old feudal notion that function is a right acquired by heredity or by consecration, and that one retains a function even when one becomes incapable of exercising it.

It was otherwise in the primitive Church. The people chose for a particular mission a man who had demonstrated that he was indeed "filled with the Spirit" (Acts 6:3). Who would dare command the Spirit, "who moves

where he pleases," to come down upon a man designated
by other men? No one has an open line to the Holy Spirit.
We must admit that ordination does not automatically
confer upon priests the talents that are necessary in the
ministry. As long as we continue to make meaningless
gestures, to pretend that the Spirit is present when it is
obvious that he is not, then we must sooner or later end
up believing that the Spirit is not present when he really
is. And this is what has happened to the Catholic Church
in the last centuries.

There will always be abuses, but it is better to have the
abuses that come from an excess of spontaneity and
vitality than those that result from mechanical behavior.
And the only way to avoid abuses altogether is to subor-
dinate the *immediate power of those who govern* to *the
ultimate authority of those who are governed.* For all
charismas, as all ministries, are conferred for the good of
the community. The community must be the judge of the
services rendered by those so endowed. No doubt, everyone receives his particular calling directly from God; but,
since it is a call to devote oneself to the common good,
it follows that this call can best be recognized and con-
trolled by those who are supposed to benefit from it.

This is pretty much what St. Paul says, when he exhorts
his people not to extinguish the Spirit, not to despise the
revelations of the prophets, but to examine everything
and to retain what is good. It is interesting to note that
this advice of Paul's, which was obviously addressed to
all the faithful and to every Christian community, was
interpreted by Vatican II, in its Constitution on the
Church, as applying only "to those who preside over the

Church." But the monopolization of authority by the hierarchy, and the absence of control from below, have so divided and so sterilized the Church that life is barely able to be communicated from the top to the bottom or from the bottom to the top.

St. John writes: "It is not every spirit, my dear people, that you can trust; test them, to see if they come from God" (I John 4:1).

What is gnawing at the Church is the spirit of clericalism. And by "clericalism" I mean the taking over by the clergy of what originally belonged to everyone. It is obvious that, in the history of Catholicism, there has been a monstrous growth of authority at the expense of the freedom of the Spirit and that of Christians.

The "gift of government" is enumerated by St. Paul among other charismas—but almost in last place, after the apostles, the prophets, the doctors, the wonder workers (who performed miracles), the healers, and the helpers. Government, in fact, appears just above glossolalia—which enables one to speak in unintelligible languages and even in sounds that are not language.

The evolution of ecclesiastical administration has caused to disappear the prophets who, along with the apostles, are the foundations of the Church (see Ephesians 2:20), and who, in the *Didache*, are called "high priests" and celebrate the Eucharist. It is their responsibility to pass on the living word of God (surely not in the style of the encyclicals), to make clear God's plan for man and his wishes, which include the liberation of the oppressed, the defense of the weak and the poor, and the satisfaction of those who thirst after justice—and not by timeless and impersonal proclamations, but by taking sides and naming names. And this, too, we lack.

With the disappearance of the prophets, the doctors (theologians and biblical scholars) have been reduced to servility before the pastors and functionaries of the Curia. They are allowed to comment on other doctors, or to repeat old doctrines, but they are not allowed to create new doctrines or even to answer questions dealing with the present time. The Church can count herself happy that more popes and bishops did not regard themselves as possessors of the gifts and functions that they denied to others. For popes and bishops easily come to believe that they have access to inspiration in all areas and in every endeavor. When they should have been listening to the prophets and the doctors, they were busy trying to replace them. They call themselves "successors of the apostles"; but they act as though they were also the successors of the prophets and doctors. Instead of educating the faithful to the voice of the Holy Spirit, they dispense them from trying to listen under the pretext that it is enough that the popes and bishops are listening.

The charismatic regime in the early Church was no doubt so vital that it must have been somewhat frightening. But St. Paul was not disturbed in the least by these uncontrolled manifestations. He admitted the miracles (which, like other manifestations, are also found outside the Church, in all fervent sects); he received the healers and helpers; and he welcomed even the glossolalists (see I Corinthians 14). For all of these charismas are able to be of service in the love and respect of the gifts of others.

Today, there is no life, no excitement, no growth, no

spontaneity. *Ubi solitudinem faciunt, pacem appellant.*
They have created a desert, and they call it peace.

But it is not only the prophets and the doctors who
have suffered at the hands of the pastors. The faithful,
too, have been despoiled of that which belonged to all of
them. In a living Church, everyone has a charisma; everyone renders service to the community; everyone is led by
the Spirit; everyone is active. Traditional Catholics are
astonished when they are told that they, too, are priests,
capable of offering spiritual sacrifices and of celebrating
the Eucharist; that they have the right to preach the
Word (I Corinthians 14:26; and Acts 4:31) and to forgive
their brothers. For many centuries, spiritual men, mar-
tyrs, and confessors of the faith claimed the right to
forgive sins. Christians confessed to laymen, to monks,
to deacons, and "from the eleventh century until the
time of Duns Scotus, exclusive of the latter, it was almost
universally accepted in Western theology that one must
confess to a layman in case of necessity."[5]

Laymen were, at one point, excluded from the liturgy
because of the use of a language and of rites that they
did not understand. They were deprived of the Bible
because the translations of it were on the Index. They
were deprived of the Eucharist, because they were "unworthy." They were denied the chalice. They were silent,
and they obeyed. They no longer participated in the government of the Church, in teaching, in the choice of
officials, or in the management of goods. Clericalism had
triumphed by establishing a sacerdotal caste into whose
hands all power had been gathered; a caste as intolerant

[5] Küng, *op. cit.*, p. 471.

and oppressive as that which was rejected by Christ and which finally killed him.

Today, the scarcity of vocations to the priesthood will deprive many faithful Christians of the Eucharist. The Church could correct this lack by ordaining fathers of families; but, instead, she will prefer her own canon law on celibacy to the divine law, which commands her to reenact the gestures of Christ and to feed her flock. Legalism had led us to this, that, once all the forms have been observed, the Holy Spirit has only to go along with what was decided for him. The truth of the matter, however, is that every ministry consists essentially in being open to the Spirit and being attentive to inspiration.

This situation is not unique to the Church. It happens whenever and wherever a regime becomes inflexible. In the socialist democracies of the East, we see the same phenomenon. The dictatorship of the proletariat, the common ownership of means of production, the exaltation of the working classes—everything is little by little transformed into a cult of personality and into bureaucratic dictatorship. Like faithful Christians going to Mass, the workers still go to their meetings. They hear repeated constantly that they are the true owners of the businesses and the true masters of the regime. And then, having cast a unanimous vote, they go home.

The real problem of every government is how to go about stirring up the interest of the people in the public good; how to go about organizing a constant exchange of men and ideas between the top and the bottom of the structure. And it is sad to observe that the government of the Church has been no more successful in this respect than was the government of Stalin.

* * *

In their defense of authority as it exists in the Church, some people will no doubt say that I am being unrealistic; that no institution can function without strong management.

What such people forget is that the Church is not a factory in which the need for production forces the workers to specialize and mechanize to the point where they become robots. The Church is not in the business of manufacturing things. It is in the business of creating men. For that purpose, it is indispensable that information be available to everyone, and that everyone participate in decisions, just as it is indispensable that everyone be educated to reflection and to the development of a truly spiritual personality.

Moreover, there is no reason to believe that management is any more efficient if it is authoritarian. Nothing is more efficacious and fruitful than a group of men working together toward a common goal. "If two of you on earth agree to ask anything at all, it will be granted to you by my Father in heaven. For where two or three meet in my name, I shall be there with them" (Matthew 18:19–20).

"Such reforms," some critics will say, "will only exchange one tyrant for another. The laity, emerging from their passivity, are often showing themselves to be more intolerant and more dictatorial than their pastors." What these people are complaining about, in effect, are the necessary consequences of the past. It is a case of the slaves suddenly being transformed into the masters; of the former colony, now independent, imitating the only model of authority that it knows. But, if the Holy Spirit is recognized as the only master of the Church, and if the charisma of government is really an ability to listen to and to communicate inspiration, then the participation by everyone in responsibility cannot possibly result in an attitude of domination and contempt.

Jesus and Authority

> "It is not right, nor wisdom, but, on the contrary, service that makes a disciple. The model for the disciple who wishes to follow Jesus is not the political leader, nor the scribe conscious of his knowledge, nor the priest who has been raised above the people (Jesus, strikingly enough, never held up the priest as a model). Only one person can be such a model; and that person is the one who serves at table. 'And I am in the midst of you as he who serves, who serves at table.' (Luke 22:27)"
>
> —Hans Kung, *The Church*, p. 542.

Jesus revolutionized the concept and the exercise of authority. For him, "power" was a temptation from Satan, and nothing surpasses the vigor with which he reprimands his Apostles when they begin bickering over the first places in the Kingdom, or when they forecast a brilliant future for him. "Get thee behind me, Satan. . . ."

What Jesus taught them above all was that the true hierarchy was not that of power, but of service: "Anyone who wants to become great among you must be your servant; and anyone who wants to be first among you must be slave to all" (Mark 10:43–44).

Among Christians, there should never be a "boss mystique" or a priestly cult. And yet, our history offers constant evidence of a tendency to sacralize force and prestige because these appear to be more effective than persuasion, freedom, and love in governing men. James and John, like us, looked forward to exercising their apostolate from thrones; and Jesus told them that, rather than thrones, they would have crosses.

Some young Latin American priests told me that when they had returned to their own countries after studying in France, they had shocked their parishioners by their desire to be simple, fraternal servants of the people. The people wanted them to keep their rank, to allow themselves to be treated as important persons—if not as sacred objects whose very touch was beneficial. It is the duty of the Church to teach people by manifesting the Spirit of God and his works in a spirit of love, brotherhood and compassion. Instead, we have chosen to subjugate them by an organization that turns them into automatons and extinguishes the Spirit in them.

If we wish to know the proper way in which to exercise authority, we have only to study Jesus. He rejects the fire-and-brimstone approach (Luke 9:55). He is tolerant

(Mark 9:38–41). He flees honors. He appeals to freedom: "If you wish to become my disciple . . . If you wish to become perfect . . . If you do this, you will be blessed. . . ." He subordinates everything to an illumination from above to which the small and the poor are open, but which human strength is incapable of producing or understanding. "It was then that, filled with joy by the Holy Spirit, he said, 'I bless you, Father, Lord of heaven and of earth, for hiding these things from the learned and the clever and revealing them to mere children. Yes, Father, for that is what it pleased you to do. Everything has been entrusted to me by my Father; and no one knows who the Son is except the Father, and who the Father is except the Son and those to whom the Son chooses to reveal him'" (Luke 10:21–22).

It is worth noting that Jesus never spoke about the dangers of anarchy; but he did have a few things to say about the authoritarianism and the ambition of the leaders of the Jews. He did not say that these leaders should govern with justice and goodness. He said that they should behave themselves as slaves; and that the man who serves most is the true master.

Only an evangelical spirit, only the Spirit of Jesus, can inspire ecclesiastical leaders to behave themselves in a manner so contrary to human nature. Concerning the proper exercise of authority, as concerning the proper use of wealth, we must say with Jesus: "To man, it is impossible; but to God, all things are possible."

Jesus, by this new teaching, contradicted not only the ambition of the apostles but also their religious beliefs. There is a close connection between the idea that we have of God and the one that we have of a human leader. We think of both spontaneously as having glory, honor, wealth, authority, prestige. But Jesus revealed a God who was gentle and humble of heart; a God who surrendered all his rights in order to be able to serve. Of the leader, he requires that he become the slave and the least of men. "Among the pagans, it is the kings who lord it over them, and those who have authority over them are given the title Benefactor. This must not happen with you" (Luke 22:25–26).

We have a natural tendency to sacralize authority, whether it be human or divine. Jesus, on the other hand, sacralized only humility and service. Therefore, his disciples may never behave like leaders. They must recognize that they become like God only in becoming humble and gentle.

The Church and Authority

"The transformation of the Church into a power structure is not a confirmation of authority, but a perversion of it. The power of the Church, as we have seen, is the power of love. The idea of power is foreign to the New Testament when it refers to authority. The Church has experienced corruption in many forms. She has known nepotism, simony, concubinage, and other vices. But these forms of corruption are perhaps

more tolerable and less dangerous to
the mission of the Church than that
which makes of the Church a means
of exercising power over other men.
The use of power, in the current
sense of imposing the will of one
being on another, is in direct
opposition to the words of Jesus
which formally and explicitly forbid
this sort of self-assertion."

—John McKenzie,
Authority in the Church

When someone asked England's John Cardinal Heenan
what, in his opinion, best characterized the Catholic
Church, he replied without hesitation: "Authority!"

Dostoyevsky's Grand Inquisitor did not put it any
better: "There are three powers on earth, and only three,
capable of overcoming forever and of winning over, for
their own good, the conscience of these helpless rebels.
These powers are the miracle, the mystery, and authority."

For many centuries, people, misled by their leaders and
indoctrinated by their priests, believed that civil authority
came directly from God. Kings were anointed, just as
bishops are still. It was necessary for philosophers and
revolutionaries to come forward, it was necessary to guil-
lotine King Louis XVI before the people could learn,
and before the Church could admit, that authority comes
from God only indirectly (in the sense that authority is
necessary), and that it belongs to the people to designate
and control the organs of authority as a social function.

For authority, like private property, *is* a social function; and, like the latter, it is unworthy of respect unless it renders a useful service.

The Church, which had adopted the languages, pomp, and titles of Europe's authoritarian regimes, refused to follow the lead of the modern states in the process of democratization. She still continues to declare that religious authority comes directly from God by way of the hierarchy; that it is God who decides, by ordination, who shall exercise that authority, just as he defines the powers of the hierarchy in the Gospel.

Obviously, there is a difference between civil authority, which is only a social necessity, and religious authority, which is based upon both social necessity and a gift of the Spirit. We have said and repeated that a pastorate is a charisma or gift, and not a simple delegation of power by the community. But the problem is to know who will be able to recognize this gift and to know how those who have it will exercise their responsibilities. And yet the imperialism of the hierarchy has progressively relieved the faithful of their right to designate their ministers and to govern themselves.

It is impossible to find in the Gospel a description of a Church organization, or of the powers of Church leaders. Jesus expressed only vaguely his plans for his successors—so vaguely, in fact, that many people have wondered whether he did not regard the end of the world as being so imminent that there would not be time, in any case, for the development of such an institution. He merely sowed the seeds that were to grow or not according to the kind of soil on which they fell; and he assembled his disciples into a community without imposing upon them a predetermined social structure.

The Old Covenant died precisely because the law of Moses contained detailed and binding instructions concerning the rites and all the laws. The faithful were smothered under this mass of rules and regulations. (Let us note in passing, and in establishing an analogy with the "traditions" of the Church, that the legislation attributed to Moses was actually composed six centuries after Moses' time.) But Jesus created a movement capable of self-adaptation and flexibility. Why, then, after having so well accommodated itself to empires, feudal structures, monarchies, and centralist government, does the Church seem unable to adapt itself to a democratic society?

The apostles, in their time, were able to organize a great diversity of communities which varied according to circumstances and did not follow a definite plan. Vatican II was obliged to correct a canon of the Council of Trent on this point which anathematized anyone "who says that in the Church there does not exist a hierarchy instituted by divine disposition and composed of bishops, priests, and ministers" (Denzinger 966). Out of respect for historical fact, the Constitution on the Church limits itself to the statement that "the ecclesiastical ministry [not the hierarchy] was instituted by divine disposition," without affirming that the division into bishops, priests, deacons, etc., goes back to the origins of the Church.

We find St. Paul, as an old man, writing pastoral epistles to ask a man—Titus, or Timothy—questions that he had asked entire communities in his major epistles. Why cannot the present-day Church, in the same spirit, return to the community all, or a part, of that which has been concentrated in the hands of one man or of several?

It is impossible to demonstrate that Christ wished the apostles to hand down their functions to their successors, or, indeed, that they themselves designated successors. It is the community, the Church as a whole, which perpetuates the mission of the apostles to whom Christ confided it, along with the means to exist and to develop —and especially the right to organize and to designate authority. The apostolicity of the Church does not consist in a legal succession of individuals who serve as a duct for grace from heaven. It consists in a living encounter between the Church as a whole and the witness of the apostles, and in faithfulness to the spirit of the apostles. The Pauline communities lived this spirit intensely, in freedom and with an abundance of charismas, and in feeling that they were repositories of the faith and of a mission. These communities were peopled by members who wished to be responsible and active. And even when it became necessary for such communities to institute a collegial or monarchical episcopate in order to combat heretics and the ills of their time, nothing was done for centuries without the consent of the people: *Quod omnes tangit, ab omnibus tractari et approbari debet.* When it is a question of the common interest, no decision can be taken unless the advice and consent of everyone is obtained. And this is the same practice followed at the first Council of Jerusalem: "Then the apostles and elders decided . . . the whole Church concurred with this" Acts 15:22).

Later, St. Ignatius would write, "Nothing can be done without the bishop. . . ." But he lived at a time when the people were still so active that there was always a danger of bypassing the bishop. Today, we must say, "Nothing can be done without the people," for the bishops are so powerful that it is the *people* who are easily bypassed.

It took many centuries for civil society to discover these same democratic principles—many centuries more than it had taken the ecclesiastical hierarchy to make the Church (the Church that had invented them) forget them. The Roman Church had had a very obvious secular tendency toward imperialism, toward absolutism, toward centralization of power, toward falsehood (the so-called Donation of Constantine, the False Decretals of the pseudo leaders), toward the abuse of excommunication, in order to establish, expand, and defend its power both temporal and spiritual. When an age of revolution deprived the Church of her states, she attempted to compensate for the loss by a proclamation of equivocal infallibility.

This sort of politics continued until Vatican II, and even afterward. The bishops have now been reduced to the role of prefects of the Pope and subjects of the Curia. When, one wonders, will we see a bishop resign because he cannot, in conscience, obey or approve of a particular doctrine? At each intervention of the Pope, they make an official protestation of their joy and their submission—and they express their reservations and objections, if at all, privately. Encyclicals and other "fallible" declarations are received with the same fearful respect as the infallible ones; and Rome attempts to translate into law what was defined only by the magisterium. No one has

ever seriously examined the case of conscience of priests
who cannot admit the doctrine set out in *Humanae vitae*.
Holding a belief contrary to that of their bishops and of
some of their faithful, what are they supposed to teach?
What are they supposed to confess? Father Pedro Arrupe,
General of the Jesuits, was still maintaining at Vatican II
that the salvation of the Church rested on *unconditional*
obedience to the Pope. Theologians are subjected to a
thousand pressures, as are teachers and biblical scholars,
to force them to recall their writings, to deny their con-
victions, to violate their consciences—all on the basis of a
decision by the Holy Office, or a decree of the Biblical
Commission, or an opinion of a Roman theologian.

Catholics are not yet free from the dehumanizing and
guilt-provoking pretensions of authority. "The Church is
a Mother, and one does not criticize one's mother. The
Pope is the Holy Father, let us not wound his heart. . . .
One owes filial trust to one's bishop." (It says "filial";
but one immediately understands that it means "infantile.") But, after all, *we* are the Church. The Church
bears us, and we bear the Church. She is as much our
daughter as she is our mother. And it is absolutely necessary for us to be able to criticize ourselves.

The Pope considers himself to be the representative
and successor of Christ, whereas he is nothing more than
the successor of Peter—and it is a succession weighted
down with errors, betrayals, and sins.

Let us say it once and for all: Authority is a function.
It must never become the object of a cult, but only of
control and collaboration.

We are now adults. We know that we cannot count on

authority to solve our problems for us. The ecclesiastical hierarchy remains the last stronghold of the old concept of substitutive and tutelary authority which pretends to purvey ready-made truths and solutions to mankind.

The Church Since Vatican II

> "The new Testament gives us the forms that authority must assume in order to make itself felt. It is not in asserting itself, but in persuading and convincing rather than in compelling, in leading rather than in dominating, in becoming personal rather than impersonal, in treating those who are governed as associates rather than as subjects, that authority makes itself felt."
>
> —John McKenzie,
> *Authority in the Church*

At the Council, the Church admitted to several errors and faults. It was a beginning; but even that rather weak beginning of reform is now threatened from all sides. The curialists are trying to recover, for the sake of the "system," the few improvements that the Council was able to tear from their hands. The timid would like to have it believed that the Church never contradicts herself—not even when she says or does something contrary to what was always understood. The conservatives say that reform is accomplished, finished. The diplomats disguise under benign formulas the scope of the revolution that is necessary. It is said, for example, that collegiality will be exercised only in decision-taking, and not in decision-making—as though it were not useless to ask for advice and then not even take that advice into account. Collegiality of consultation is meaningless without a collegiality of government.

It is also said, "It is not a matter of attacking the nature of authority, but only the way in which authority is exercised." That too is obviously false. The nature of a being determines the way in which it acts; and the main question at the moment is how to define the difference between the nature of authority in the Church and in civil society.

What it boils down to is that some people are trying to preserve the reality of dictatorship by granting ephemeral concessions on matters of no importance. But the iron hand, whether or not it is gloved in velvet, remains nonetheless antievangelical. If the voice of Rome has become as sweet as that of Jacob, its hand remains nonetheless the hand of Esau—the hand that struck Lemercier, Illich, Schillebeeckx, Cardonnel, Oraison, Halbfas, Besret, Oosterhuis, and Girardi.

Everyone is talking today about "service." But it is pointed out, subtly enough, that a servant is not the same as a flunky. And, somehow, we see these new "servants" as wielding the same authority that they did when they were "masters."

The essential distinction is that a servant is not master of himself and his acts, nor the final judge of the value

of his service. He has no right to impose himself upon his
master. Obviously, one must grant a good servant the
right to act on his own initiative, and even, if the master's true interests require it, to displease his employers
and contradict them. In such cases, the master must trust
the servant enough to rely on his common sense, and he
must take account of his advice and even of his moods.
All of this, however, is based, not on the right of the
servant to serve, but upon the consent of the master—a
consent that can be justified by the value of the service
rendered. Without that consent and without such value,
there is no longer a servant; there is only a domestic
tyrant.

The Roman theologians and the conservative bishops
are concerned with preserving the "freedom" of the Pope
against the encroachments of collegiality. But a servant
is not free to interpret and exercise his function according
to his own wishes. To the contrary, he must serve in accordance with the wishes of others; and above all he
must serve to the satisfaction of his master—the people
of God, in this case.

Vatican I placed certain limits on the pontifical power
in stating, in the *Acts* of the Council, that such power
was not absolute or arbitrary. But these limitations are
inoperable so long as it remains true that *Sancta Sedes a
nemine judicatur*—"there is no appeal from the Holy See"
—and so long as there remains no control on the exercise
of the papal office. It is disastrous for a society not to
have any recourse against dictatorship other than anarchy
—as we have seen in the case of *Humanae vitae*.

The true proprietor of power in the Church is the whole

of the Church; and the delegation of authority to the
hierarchy must ever remain subject to the final approval
of the Church as a whole. The court of final appeal is
neither the episcopal college nor the Pope, but the faith
of believers who must be able to recognize themselves in
the declarations, and especially in the conduct, of the
hierarchy.

Infallibility

> "Catholics are not surprised to learn
> that the authority of the Church is
> human. But they are surprised when
> they are told that authority is
> actually superhuman, and that it is
> therefore free to act in a thoroughly
> human way."
>
> —John McKenzie,
> *Authority in the Church*

The heart of the problem of authority in the Church lies
in papal infallibility.

As someone has said, man is infallibly fallible. What,
then, can we possibly mean when we say that the Pope
is infallible?

The Pope has the benefit of a "special assistance" from
the Holy Spirit—an assistance that is not an "inspiration,"
and even less a magical power. This assistance is available to a pope in his studies, reflections, and consultations;
but it does not replace these things, and even less does it

replace a pope's honesty and intelligence. If he acts out of pride, stubbornness or presumption, there is nothing to prevent him from making an error. How can we possibly think otherwise?

Modern theologians are trying, a bit belatedly, to minimize the meaning of this exorbitant prerogative of infallibility. They point out that the Pope cannot "engage the plenitude of his authority against the consensus of the episcopal body" (Reverend H. Bouillard). But they forget to explain how that situation would be resolved and who would be the final judge in such a case. The ecumenists rejoice over the decree of Vatican II which recalls that there is a certain order, a hierarchy of values among the truths of Catholic doctrine, and that the Assumption of Mary and the primacy of Peter are not on the same level as the dogmas relating to Christ or to the Trinity. This, however, seems a rather shabby satisfaction; for how can a pope be more or less infallible?

If we reflect upon the meaning of the concept, if we study the history of the Church, we will arrive at an infinitely better understanding of what this infallibility is, whether we are talking about the Pope or about the Church as a whole. Infallibility, obviously, does not mean that one is free from fault (that would be impeccability), or even that one is free from error (as witnessed by numerous examples from history). The theologians who wrote the minority opinion for the Commission on Birth Control said this: "If the Church has erred so gravely and in such a way as seriously to engage its responsibility for the conduct of souls, this would be tantamount to a serious insinuation that the assistance of the Holy Spirit was lacking." No doubt, one can find innumerable such cases—where the assistance of the Holy Spirit was present, but where it was nullified by the resistance of churchmen. For example: the excommunication of the Greek Church; the prohibition against lending money at interest; the condemnation of Galileo; the quarrel over rites that resulted in the failure of the missions; the secular persecution of Jews; intolerance; support of the Pope's secular power; the condemnation of historical criticism; the condemnation of the theory of evolution, and so forth.

The theologians of the majority answer prudently: "The criteria which allow one to distinguish what the Holy Spirit may have permitted from what he may not have permitted are *a priori* difficult to determine. We know, in effect, that there have been errors in the preaching of the magisterium and in tradition. . . ."

To sustain the infallibility of the Pope and of the Church, in the strict sense of the term, would be the equivalent of making a perpetual miracle of ecclesiastical history. The only acceptable meaning of infallibility is that of God's indefectibility with respect to the Church —an indefectibility which it has pleased some to confuse with the Church's indefectibility with respect to God. It is not the Church which is faithful to God, but God who is faithful to the Church. God will never abandon the Church; the Holy Spirit will never let the Church rest in its errors, but, with inexhaustible patience, will inspire her with sorrow for her faults and with a determination to correct her errors.

This, it seems (despite a few moments of timidity), is the concept of Hans Küng: "In the future, should we not, basing ourselves upon Scripture, consider ecclesial infallibility as residing less in certain propositions or doctrines than in the conviction of faith according to which the Spirit of God maintains and never ceases to renew the Church, despite all errors and through all errors of popes, bishops, theologians, pastors, men and women?"

And Karl Rahner, in his report to the International Commission of Theologians of October 1969, warns us, "If, today, the magisterium of the Church does not find the courage and the daring to delete its foregoing errors, it will no longer be worthy of our faith and trust."

The best indication of God's indefectibility, however, is found in our own daily experience of the way in which the Spirit acts in each one of us who are the Church: convicting us of our sins, flushing us out of our hiding places, leading us, terrified, "there where we do not wish to go." As it happens within each individual member of the Church, so it happens for the Church as a whole. And God is taking odds that there will always be a sufficient number of loving hearts among us, and of open minds, for his inspiration to be welcomed and for his Word to be assured of an answer.

*　　*　　*

If Catholics succeed in understanding infallibility in the sense described above—that is, not as an element of oppression or as a means of infantile security, but as a collective means of continuing renewal—then they will be free, and they will make authority free also. For authority, as the world has seen in the case of *Humanae vitae*, is itself a prisoner of outdated proclamations. This is true even though authority is capable, when it seems to serve a useful purpose, of conveniently forgetting some of those rather embarrassing proclamations. Who remembers today, for example, that Leo X condemned the proposition, "It is contrary to the will of the Spirit that heretics be burned"; or that Pius IX, in 1864, declared that the Church should "exercise, until the end of time, its empire, not only over men but also over nations and their supreme heads." Or that Pius X spoke of "that eminently pernicious doctrine which holds that the laity is an element of progress in the bosom of the Church."

The trouble is that the Church intoxicated herself with the notion of sacredness, and declared to be sacred everything in sight. (In the Pope's entourage, everything is holy or sacred. There is even a Bank of the Holy Spirit in Rome.) And the Pope perpetuated this oversacralization by surrounding himself with the pomp and splendor of a Renaissance court. The papal household, from hearing constant references to its omniscience, holiness, and sacredness, ended up by believing its own publicity and thus losing contact with reality. Not long ago, we were offered a remarkable example of the "progress" that is being made in Rome: the Pope reformed his household. The inevitable result of such a tiny step in the right direction, however, is that the faithful are scandalized to discover how much the papal court was in need of reformation, and how much this first attempt had to leave untouched.

It is only through regular contact with the faithful, with ordinary Christians, that Church authorities can be brought to a more realistic, and more modest, opinion of themselves. Then, instead of an aristocratic Church, in which the Pope is regarded as "the head, the cornerstone, the root, the source, and the origin of all authority and power," a Church in which the Pope has "full and universal jurisdiction," a Church in which the Pope is the "visible principle of faith and communion" (Vatican I), we will have a Church that conforms both to the Gospel and to the needs of the time. It will be a democratic Church in which all authority will rest with the people of God, and in which the people of God will have every ministry at its disposal.

What I have described is a revolution. But it is a revolution that has already begun.

The Council has proclaimed: "Let us allow to the faithful, to both clerics and laymen, a just freedom of research and of thought, and a just freedom to let their opinions be known, humbly and courageously, in areas in which they are competent."[6]

Those are fine words. But, as it turns out, neither the Council itself, nor the Episcopal Synod, was capable of obtaining for itself the liberty that it wished for the faithful. Pope Paul forbade any discussion of birth control and clerical celibacy. And when a certain cardinal acted as though he took the Council's words seriously with respect to courageous laymen, he was reprimanded by the Pope, and condemned by the Dean of the Sacred College as well as by the cardinals who were regarded (by Roman standards) as being progressive. One can only guess at what the "conservative" cardinals thought and wrote about the matter.

[6] Constitution on the Church in the World, p. 62.

Ecclesiastical Functions

Over the centuries, ecclesiastical functions have been modeled after civil functions—so much so that, carrying this tendency to a ridiculous extreme, the legislative, executive, and judicial prerogatives of Christ the King have been described in great detail.

If we read the Gospel, however, we find a wholly different approach to these functions.

1. *To Teach*

The Church must teach, not by compelling people to learn, but by persuading them. Christians know that the only master of truth is the Spirit. The Spirit cannot be replaced by the formulas of the "magisterium of the Church"; rather, the magisterium must learn to listen and to recognize, from what the Church says on the outside, what the Spirit is saying on the inside. The true apostle has the gift of meditation and illumination; and those who possess that gift are the ones who are chosen by the community to exercise it.

A Christian must, of course, assent to the Revelation of Jesus Christ. But if a man cannot bring himself to accept a particular dogma, this does not mean that he must be excluded from the communion of the faithful —so long as he himself does not attempt to exclude those who differ from him. Instead, such a man should be allowed to continue searching until, with the passage of time, he is able to see matters in the same light as his brothers. The practical application of this is that the Church must give up its barbarous principle of "all or nothing." The Church herself took centuries to build up her Credo; and yet, she requires that a convert adopt it instantly, and that every Christian adhere to it totally. If we are at all concerned about sincerity of belief, then we must admit the existence of a differential and progressive adhesion to the articles of faith.

To excommunicate someone for a difference in the articulation of belief is an authoritarian practice analogous to civil banishment; as such, it should never have been permitted in the Church, for it has led only to wars and irreparable schisms. To love one another means to be able to bear one another's differences. Unity among the faithful is not supposed to result in doctrinal or disciplinary unanimity, but in a love which overcomes diversity and in adherence to Christ and his Word.

From the beginning of its history, the Church has suffered immeasurably from its passion for debating, defining, and anathematizing. It is difficult to understand how it can be useful to try to resolve questions before truth has had a chance to ripen in the minds of men by means of dialogue, reflection, and the passage of time. What is important, in other words, is not what the head of the Church believes, but what the members of the Church believe—the faith of the people of God. So long as the people of God do not see their own beliefs reflected in an official formulation, then that formulation is premature, and the question should be allowed to rest and ripen for a longer period of time. What the Church should have done for "heretics," therefore, was not to condemn them, but to teach them to respect "orthodox" opinions by setting an example and respecting the opinions of the heretics. Then, in the atmosphere of peace and tolerance which would have resulted, it would have been possible to exchange ideas until the problem, if possible, had been resolved.

In this area, as in so many others, the Church lost in influence what she gained in authority. The hierarchy became absorbed in measures of control and repression; it chose, in other words, to become a brake rather than a stimulus. It thought, for many centuries, that its definitions were identified with truth. But the contemporary discovery of the relativity of our formulas must now forbid us to condemn those who do not admit those formulas.

But, if all this is so, who or what is the final authority on matters of truth? It seems to me that the answer is self-evident. The final and supreme authority cannot be either the individual or the community, for both are fallible; it can only be truth itself.

That answer is not as much a begging of the question as it may seem. It means that truth must be sought, and sought with perseverance. The only guarantee of progress is to listen to and consult everyone who is alive and who thinks. Truth is not the property of anyone, but, if I had to give practical directions for finding it, I would say that, at any given time and in any given place, it lies in the formulation that is capable of gaining the assent of the greatest number of people because it enlightens them, improves them, and seems to them to represent obvious and durable progress with respect to what they believed earlier.

2. To Administer the Sacraments

The sacraments are gifts or charismas the existence of which is evident to the community, and which the community utilizes by designating those who possess those gifts as their ministers.

There is a charisma for the breaking of bread, which allows the one who has it to awaken love and thanksgiving, and profound and joyful communication, among members of a community and with Christ.

There is a charisma of forgiveness, which creates a mood of humility in a community, an exchange of confidence and respect by means of which the members are unburdened of their sins and their despair and made cognizant of what is best in themselves.

There is a charisma of love and of marriage which symbolizes the love of Christ for the Church; a charisma of healing the sick; a charisma of discerning the presence of the Spirit—and many others, all given by Jesus to his Church.

None of these gifts, however, are created by the sacraments. The sacraments are only the signs and symbols of them. Without faith, for example, there is no baptism; without love, there is no marriage; without repentance, there is no forgiveness; and without a true community, there is no Real Presence. We should prefer a faith without baptism to a baptism without faith; a love without marriage to a marriage without love; a community with-

out the Mass to a Mass without a community; and repentance without absolution to absolution without repentance.

It is no doubt desirable that the gifts of God be
celebrated, signified, authenticated. The trouble is that
we have reached the point in the Church where we
believe that the sacraments replace and create the human
realities to which actually they only correspond. The
sacraments, in reality, are only the signs of the presence
of these gifts, and the sacraments can therefore exist
only because the gifts existed prior to them.

3. *To Govern*

Every society has need of at least a minimum of co-
ordination and order. And the Church needs more than a
minimum. Thus, the job of governing requires a special
gift or charisma. That gift does not consist, however, in
the right to impose the decisions of the leader on the
members of the community, but in a talent for establishing communication and understanding. The leader is not
the man who gives the orders, but the man who is able
to create an atmosphere of faith, love, and respect, and
to establish a community of views and aspirations in
such a way that the solutions to problems are discovered
in a spirit of moral unanimity.

In normal circumstances, the function of governing is
exercised collegially—which means not that decisions will
be arrived at by majority vote, but that the leaders
should first understand and persuade one another, as
they are supposed to be capable of doing for the other
members of the community, so that they may create an

atmosphere of truth and love which will elicit the consent of the community as a whole.

What happens if that consent is not forthcoming? Isn't it necessary at that point to have a supreme authority who can resolve the question? It seems to me that a supreme authority entails more disadvantages than advantages. To those who would justify the existence of the classical papacy by citing its accomplishments in

In normal circumstances, the function of governing is unifying the Church, I would reply that the preoccupation with unifying and centralizing the Church was the principal factor in the two catastrophic divisions that have rent the Body of Christ: the Eastern Schism, and Protestantism.

Finally, I must add that solutions imposed by authority are worth absolutely nothing so far as one's conscience goes. Such solutions may serve to beat a sick man into submission, but they cannot cure his disease.

*   *   *

Here is an interesting suggestion. Some people, among them the English author Anthony Spencer, have suggested that the Church's governing mission be broken down into the same divisions as those of modern states. There would be an "expressive" function, and an "instrumental" function. The first would symbolize the unity and the spirit of the Church; and the second—which it would be well not to confound or compromise with the first—would be in charge of adapting the fundamental values of the Church to the evolution of civilization.

Thus, the Pope and the bishops would become presidents, or at least constitutional monarchs; and, presumably, they would designate cabinet ministers who would assume responsibility for measures that might be unpopular. The community as a whole would be given the opportunity, at regular intervals, to express their confidence or lack of confidence both in the men in power and in their policies.

At present, says Mr. Spencer, the opposite is happening. Those who make controversial decisions remain anonymous and hide behind the skirts of papal authority. Instead of this, the Pope and the bishops should normally follow the advice received from the leaders of different schools of thought, so that their leadership may continue to enjoy the general confidence of the Church.

What Mr. Spencer is saying, in effect, is that the machinery of ecclesiastical government is now in trouble and poorly maintained, and that it needs repairs desperately.

*   *   *

The reforms suggested above could be completed only by decentralization and localization of authority. The more a democracy is direct, the more it is vital. Life does not emanate from a central organization; but centralization renders local efforts ineffectual—as can be seen today in the local churches, which are being held on a leash by the Holy See.

It seems that a double movement is taking shape. There is a need for decentralization with respect to Rome. The local churches want to recover their initiative and their identity. They are asking that decisions be made at the level most directly in touch with their problems, and that the central authority intervene only when local authority is either incapable of action or unwilling to act. There is also a need for the regrouping of bishops into national conferences. It would be disastrous, however, if these conferences assumed the functions of parliaments or of government administrations. The function of the bishop, after all, is an essential one. Bishops have strayed far from their true function—so far, in fact, that Christians rarely look to them nowadays for spiritual nourishment, direction, and guidance. As the bishop's role as governor was taken over by the Curia, he relinquished his pastoral role to the parish priests. In order for them now to recover that latter function, the number of bishops must be multiplied, and there must be a bishop for every town and city and for every suburb of the larger cities—just as there was in other times.

＊   ＊   ＊

When, at Vatican II, it was decided to define the Church not by the hierarchy but by the people of God, no one, very likely, was aware of the scope of the revolution that that definition would entail. Up to that time, the Church had marched, so to speak, on its head. Now, it has to use its feet. What is important now is not to replace old structures with new ones, but that the Church begin to move. As it does so, life itself will create the structures that are needed—structures that will have to be cast off when they are no longer serviceable. What does it really matter if not a stone remains upon a stone in the temple in which we were raised? The Spirit has only one abode: living man. "Didn't you realize that you were God's temple and that the Spirit of God was living among you? If anybody should destroy the temple of God, God will destroy him, because the temple of God is sacred; and you are that temple" (I Corinthians 3:16–17).

Chapter Three

Christianity Without Religion

CONTEMPORARY THEOLOGICAL DEBATE CENTERS ON THIS QUESTION: Did Jesus intend to found a religion, or did he abolish all religions? In other words, is Christianity the worship of God, or is it a human service, a devotion or dedication? Has the priesthood of the faithful delivered us from the hands of the priests, or has the Church been correct in establishing a hierarchy of "sacred" pastors leading a "flock" of laymen? Did Christ abolish all sacrifices, or did he institute the "daily sacrifice" of the Mass?

We must begin by admitting that the New Testament is surprisingly nonresponsive on these points, as on so many others. Jesus introduced so many new things that his disciples were unable to assimilate them all at once and draw the logical conclusions from them. They mixed in their own ideas with his, articulated his innovations within the framework for which these ideas were not intended, preserved the old Hebrew wineskins alongside the new wine of the Gospel.

Who, in reading the works of the evangelists, can say for sure whether or not Jesus believed that the end of the world was imminent? Did he believe that his own generation would see the Parousia (Matthew 10:23; Mark 9:1 and 13:30; Luke 21:32), or did he actually intend to found a Church? What is certain is that the first generation of Christians was mistaken on this point —which is a proof that the teaching they had received was not clear to them.

Did Jesus intend to work miracles or not?

Was he or was he not the equal of God?

What kind of poverty was he referring to in the Beatitudes? Was it economic poverty, or the spiritual virtue of poverty?

No one can answer these questions clearly and decisively. And no matter what answer one accepts, there are always texts in support of the contrary opinion.

Our problem is still more complex: Did Jesus abolish the religion of Israel, or did he merely perfect it? His own words on that subject appear contradictory. Sometimes, he seems to regard himself as a preserver: "not one dot, not one little stroke, shall disappear from the Law . . ." (Matthew 5:18), and he strongly reprimanded the scribes and Pharisees (Matthew 23:23) for having "neglected the weightier matters of the Law." At other times, he sounds like a revolutionary, correcting the law of Moses (Matthew 19:8), setting himself up in opposition to tradition "You have learned how it was said to our ancestors . . . But I say this to you . . ." (Matthew 5:21), and openly ignoring the law of sabbatical repose and the alimentary prohibitions for which many Jews gave up their lives because to do otherwise would have been equivalent to apostasy (Mark 7:14).

In view of the discussions of the primitive Church and the somewhat lame decision of Acts (15:18)—which, it seems, Paul never did apply—we are compelled to search for a principle that frees us from such compromises.

Let us go one step further and put the question this way: Did Jesus institute a religion—a hierarchy, rites,

laws? Or did he order his disciples to preach the good
news that there were no more castes, no more intermediaries between God and us, no law other than that
of love, no more chasm between priest and layman,
between the scholar and the simple man, between rich
and poor, between man and woman, between the sacred
and the profane; that God no longer wished to be honored
at Jerusalem and at Garizim by grandiose cults and
specialized priests, but that he was looking for men
who would worship him in spirit and in truth and who
would honor him everywhere and forever?

In order to find the answer to all these questions in
the Gospel, we will have to interpret the words of the
evangelists in trying to disengage the original meaning
of Christ from the limitations and changes imposed upon
it by the mentality and environment of the time.

In an area like this one, where one is tempted to
react at an emotional level, we must begin by a definition
of terms. Such definitions are the only way that we can
succeed in understanding one another, and perhaps even
in reaching agreement.

A *religion*, first of all, is an ensemble of practices,
concepts, precepts, and ministers by means of which man
attempts to enter into relations with God. Pagans, terrified
by their isolation in nature, try anxiously to find security
by binding themselves to a supernatural that must be
appeased, conciliated, and pacified. Their worship is a
public and ritualistic expression of that attitude. The religious spirit among pagans places its trust in consecrated
men, in rites, in sacrifices. It is addressed to a god who

demands temporal tribute, praise, money, and victims in exchange for grace.

Christianity, on the other hand, represents an initiative on the part of God to communicate himself to man —a free gift that man may accept freely in order to transmit it to his brothers. Man does not even have to be concerned about returning the gift to God, for God wants nothing for himself, and he counts as having been done for himself anything that is done for the least of his people.

The God of the Christians is so incredibly new that we are constantly deforming him by trying to force him into concepts that predate him. We try to make him resemble the Yahweh of the Jews, the Unmoved Mover of Aristotle, or the Idea of Plato.

We all act as though we know God perfectly well —and then we try to verify the revelation of Christ by means of our philosophies. But Christ himself said that no one knows the Father except the Son. And, to Jews who had behind them two thousand years of instruction in "revealed religion," he dared to say, "You say, 'He is our God,' although you do not know him. But I know him, and if I were to say: I do not know him, I should be a liar, as you are liars yourselves" (John 8:54-55).

Rather than accept the dizzying originality of God as revealed by Jesus, we have chosen to rationalize him; or, at best, we have juxtaposed his message alongside our philosophy. For how can we reconcile an Almighty God with a God of Love? (Someone once asked: "What did Jesus do during earthquakes and floods?") How can

we reconcile the Omnipotent Judge with the father of
the prodigal son; the God who creates for his own
glory with a Jesus who is meek and humble of heart;
the Lord and Master with the one who does not choose
to be served, but rather to serve (Mark 10:45; Acts
17:25), to suffer and to sacrifice himself. Obviously, we
cannot have both. We must choose one or the other.

In order to believe in the God whom Jesus revealed on
the cross ("Who sees me, sees the Father"), it is not
enough to add a few theses to our philosophy books.
We must enter into a personal dialogue that will allow
us to understand the wishes and the paradoxical beatitudes
of this unimaginable God. Then and only then will we
be able to understand the possibility that this revolutionary God has suppressed religion (i.e., his rights and
our duties to him) in order to devote himself and ourselves wholeheartedly to men.

To worship a God-Dominator is equivalent to creating
a hierarchical Church and a caste society. Even our
liturgy reflects and consecrates a society of classes and
thus reinforces the acquiescence of the people in the
status quo rather than liberating them from it. But to
love a God who makes himself the least of creatures
and the servant of all, this is the way to establish a
community of brothers in which man is saved from solitude, and freed from subjection and exploitation both
active and passive.

*   *   *

Another essential characteristic of all religions is a fundamental division between the sacred and the profane;
that is, between the domain in which man is free to

pursue inoffensive occupations, and that in which the slightest digression can cause him to be lost, and in which rectitude guarantees his salvation. Religion teaches man how to behave in the domain of the sacred. Thus, religion divides human life into two sectors, divides man into two classes and encourages him to act at two levels, and excuses his passivity in this world by his mysterious participation in the other world.

Christianity in its pure state knows of no such divisions. For Christians, since the moment that God became man, the sacred has resided in the profane. The whole of human life must be sanctified, and not only certain places, certain persons, and certain moments. Christianity is not intended to reveal the secrets of the worship of God, but to reveal the sacred character of man—of all men— and to demonstrate that there is no way to reach God except by serving one's brothers. God cannot be found in a temple or in a ritual. We can approach him only by means of human relations and through the development of our own humanity. There is no special area of creation reserved to God; everything has been placed under man's domination.

Christ systematically desacralized everything that, in his time, was considered sacred. He desacralized the temple: "Destroy this Temple . . ." he said. "You will worship the Father neither on this mountain nor in Jerusalem" (John 4:21). St. Paul and St. Stephen preached constantly "against the Law and the Holy Place" (Acts 6:14–15, 7:48). He desacralized the priests, and he preferred heretics who served their brothers to them. He desacralized ascetic practices, the fine distinctions between "pure" and "impure," and religious fasts by describing them all as "old wineskins" (Matthew 9:17). He desacralized worship by telling his followers that before they worshiped they must first go and be reconciled with their brothers, and by insisting that mercy was more important than sacrifice. He even desacralized the sabbath, the sacred day *par excellence* instituted and respected by God himself. "The sabbath was made for man, and not man for the sabbath" (Mark 2:27).

He taught that the only things really sacred were those that were most ordinary and most profane: man, the laity, the people, the poor. If one seeks to be filled with God, it is useless to frequent the temples, to know the words of the rituals and the magical gestures. It avails one nothing to use priests as intermediaries or to offer sacrifices. What one must do is love one's fellow men, respect them. Religion is no longer a refuge from history. Christianity is rather the commitment of God to the liberation of man.

If we want to appreciate the radical originality of Christianity with respect to the religion of the Jews and all other religions, we have only to recall the extent to which Jesus scandalized the most devoted worshipers of Yahweh. He was not a priest[1]; he had no religious au-

---

[1] Christ never spoke of the priesthood nor of a cult of worship except in critical terms. He never called himself a priest, nor did he refer to his disciples by that title. The New Testament establishes that Christ offered a perfect sacrifice which abolished all sacrifices and all priesthoods. It is an infinitely significant fact that, in the New Testament as in the writings of the apostolic and postapostolic fathers, the Greek word *hiereus* (which signifies a properly sacerdotal function), is always used to designate Christ or the faithful, but never the ministers that we call priests or bishops. Such ministers were designated by more strictly functional names: "elders"; "supervisors"; "presidents."

thority; and as a layman he raised himself up against a priestly caste and against a religion founded and organized by God himself. He respected no hierarchy. He abolished all mediation. He claimed a directly divine origin, and he challenged the most sacred ties. (Who is my mother? he asked. Who are my brothers? Who are my neighbors? And the answer he gave was that it was not the priest or the Levite, but the charitable heretic.) And he did all this by proclaiming universal brotherhood.

It was a great scandal, and one which was visited upon the early Christians by those most religious men who despised and taunted them by asking, "What is this new sect? Where are your temples, where are your priests, where are your sacrifices? There is nothing religious to you. You are atheists." And the Christians answered proudly. "Yes, we are atheists so far as your false gods are concerned, your gods hidden away in your temples, served by your priests, and nourished by your sacrifices. We are all priests, and we offer to God the spiritual sacrifice of our whole lives [I Peter 2:5, Romans 12:1]. We are the true temple of our God, who does not live among stones but in the hearts of men. We break and share bread in our houses, in joy and simplicity, so that there are no poor among us."

And yet, two centuries later, under Judeo-pagan influence, the Christians had adopted everything that they had rejected earlier. They began building sumptuous temples that they dared call "houses of God." They multiplied the "sacred orders." They organized solemn and mysterious liturgies which, they thought, placed them

in communication with God. And they stopped sharing
among themselves. The old God, the Boss, the Omnipotent egocentric, had regained his place—and, naturally,
the poor man had regained his.

*   *   *

For centuries, the Church prospered at the level of
natural religiosity. It became a religion among other
religions, a religion like other religions, instead of remaining the religion that was able to reconcile all religions in the love and respect of man directly inspired
by God.

The clericalization of the Church, in giving to the clergy
what had belonged to everyone (the priesthood, proph-
esy, preaching, the forgiveness of sins), was the most
important factor in de-Christianizing the Church. The
faithful were turned into a proletariat; and there were
many among them who had such a taste for liberty,
dignity, and responsibility—that is, who had a taste for
Christ—that they could not be Christians in such a Church.

The Church and the hierarchy became indistinguish-
able one from the other. The sacred character of the
hierarchy was exalted (the Most Holy Father, the Sacred Congregations, the Sacred Purple, the Sacred Laws),
and it was set apart from the rest of the faithful according to the pagan custom of separating the wheat from
the chaff, the sacred from the profane. Originally, men
had been placed in the service of God, and this allowed
them to be placed in the service of the Church. But
then the Church, whose natural boundaries are the world
itself, became occupied solely with herself, consecrated
herself to the preservation of her power and her goods,

and confined herself to the domain of the sacred. It reached the point where geographic withdrawal from the world was said to be the surest means of salvation. It was taught that man sanctified himself principally by prayer and the sacraments, and Christianity was measured by the number of times that one went to Mass, to communion, and to confession. God, in effect, seemed to have placed salvation in the hands of the hierarchy to do with as it wished. The hierarchy could give communion to the faithful, or excommunicate them, as though it were able to read the hearts of men. The Lord's Supper was no longer the community feast of the whole of the priestly people, for the Church had now been purged of such profane and gross concerns as food and sharing; it was now a sacrifice that was offered to God to appease him and reconcile him with us. It was forgotten that it is God who sacrifices himself ("God in Christ was reconciling the world to himself" [II Corinthians 5:19]); that it is not God who must be reconciled with humanity, but man who must be reconciled with God by means of an initiative on God's part. "It is all God's work. It was God who reconciled us to himself through Christ" (II Corinthians 5:18 and Colossians 1:20).

*   *   *

The reaction to this situation began with Vatican II. We can appreciate the importance of that Council's revolution when we understand that, in defining the Church as the People of God, the Church was secularized. It has become, above all, the laity; and all the rest (the rites, the Credo, the hierarchy) are only the means by which the laity is served.

The Council compelled the Church to go back to the original concept of Christianity by reestablishing the validity of the priesthood of the faithful and the spiritual worship that every man is expected to render in his daily life: "All their activities, their prayers and their apostolic undertakings, their conjugal and family life, their recreation of mind and body, if they are lived in the Holy Spirit—and also the trials of life, if they are patiently accepted—all these things become 'spiritual sacrifices, which Jesus Christ has made acceptable to God' (I Peter 2:5)."[2]

This effectively rejects every division between the sacred and the profane. Henceforth, everything is sacred and is penetrated by love.

In the light of this attitude, we should no longer be surprised at the present crisis of the clergy. If all Christians are priests for the whole of their lives, if the priesthood has been laicized and the laity sacralized, what need is there for a sacred priesthood that is not part of the laity? The traditional priest—the repository of the sacred, the mediator between the world of God and the world of man—has no place in the postcounciliar Church.

*   *   *

This interpretation of Christianity is so self-evident that it is somewhat disturbing. How on earth could we have gone so far astray in past centuries? There must be an internal cause that made us err so seriously on the nature of Jesus' revelation.

[2] *Lumen gentium*, p. 34.

There is, in fact, such a cause, and it is found in the fact that, even in primitive Christianity, there were elements of religion: apostolic authority, preaching, baptism, a symbol of faith (*Credo*), the Eucharist, regulations and rules. These are all "religious" elements in the sense that they are things that lie outside ordinary life and outside man's ordinary occupations; things that tend to establish a distinction between the sacred and the profane.

This development, however, is neither inevitable nor irreversible. Elements of religion do not necessarily transform Christianity into a religion. Everything depends on the way these elements are conceived and on the way in which they are used. In this respect, there are several things to note:

1. All Catholics admit that such elements are only means of serving the faithful. They become perverted only if the "structures" become so heavy that they suffocate those who use them, and only if they become so important that they retain what is sacred for themselves rather than spreading it over the whole of Christian life. After Vatican II, who still defines a Christian as someone who goes to Mass? And who is not aware of the extent to which the sacraments are no longer frequented?

2. These elements, which are called "sacred" (i.e., devoted to God's service), cannot be "holy" (i.e., filled with love). But, on the other hand, what is profane can overflow with holiness. True Christianity is characterized by that subordination of the sacred.

3. These religious elements are not indispensable to salvation. The Council affirmed that salvation was open

to all men. Only faith can save, and faith is given to God, who shows himself and offers himself to every man without making use of a specialized mediary, and even without requiring conscious reflection or conceptual expression.

4. These elements or means should not become obligations centered around the rights of God or of the worship of God. They remain Christian only so long as they remain in the service of man, so long as they spread the good news of our liberation from religion by a God who wishes to be the least of us and the servant of all.

The originality of Christianity lies in this, that the ceremonies which are superficially the most "religious" are basically focused on man and on life. They are not "sacred" rites that turn our attention to another world; they are human gestures which reveal and operate the sanctification of daily life—of meals, reconciliations, familial or social commitments.

The Eucharist is not a sacrifice offered to God. It is a commemoration of Christ's devotion to his brothers. It makes Christ present among us by uniting his members in brotherhood to share bread in memory of him.

By transforming this sacrifice of God to man into a sacrifice by man to God, we have ritualized it. And, in so doing, we have lost sight of its most important meaning, of that joyful and surprising news that God himself has freed us from our religious obligations and united us to our brothers through the love that he communicates to us.

Jesus never ordered us to reenact the "sacrifice of the cross." He merely recommended that we renew his last meal with his brothers. A "religious mentality" chose to interpret that as a repetition of the holy sacrifice of the cross, from which the aspect of a meal had been exorcised (as being too profane, no doubt). Thus, the Lord's Supper was dehumanized so that it might be divinized —which is the exact opposite of what Christianity is supposed to do.

Similarly, the sacraments of baptism and penance are not a sort of magical purification, but a work of reconciliation, a sharing of forgiveness which unites us to God by uniting us to one another, and which brings God's forgiveness to us by making us forgive one another.

The sacraments are gifts which brothers give to one another. They care for the sick, comfort the dying, aid and encourage married couples, and confer a mission upon those who are chosen. Thus, the New Covenant, far from being a worship of God, consists essentially in the daily life of Christians animated by the Holy Spirit. Earthly reality is referred to God even without the sacraments, without conscious prayer, in a purely secular way; that is, through love, which pervades all the acts of a Christian.

It is necessary, of course, that a Christian be mindful of Jesus and be filled with him. But the best way to accomplish this is for him to maintain the same theocentric and anthropocentric orientation as Christ; that is, to love God in the service of man.

The ministers of true Christianity are not the organizers of worship, the distributors of the sacraments, but the preachers of the good news that we have all been given free and direct access to God through the least of our brothers. It will always be necessary, no doubt, to have someone to preside over the assembly of the people of God; but this can be anyone, or the people can take turns, or it can be someone who has a special talent for it.[3]

The Christian community is centered neither on God nor on itself. It is dedicated to the service of the world. An assembly of Christians is always adjourned by a dismissal, a sending out of the faithful on a mission. The purpose of the Church is not to regiment men, but to liberate them from all oppression, even religious oppression, in the name of Jesus the Universal Liberator.

The more these elements are laicized, the more they will unify human life and the more they will become Christian. As paradoxical as it may seem, a religion which centers on God in order to praise him, appease him and ask him for favors, is a purely human religion. Christianity, on the other hand, is divine because it reveals a God who is not made in our image; a God who is a gift, love, the pouring out and diffusion of himself, a God whom man is incapable of inventing.

[3] "Investigation of the Pauline organization of the Church has revealed that it is possible to have a charismatic community order without special investiture for the rendering of service (i.e., ordination). At Corinth, for example, there were no supervisors, no elders, and no ordination of any kind. With the exception of the Apostle, all charismas were spontaneously generated. In spite of that, the Church of ordination of any kind. With the exception of the Apostle, all charismas were spontaneously generated. In spite of that, the Church of Corinth had everything that it needed. There was a full measure of preaching of the Word, Baptism, the Eucharist, all the services" (Küng, *The Church*, pp. 607–8).

This by no means denies the legitimacy of a more developed organization with priests and bishops, so long as that organization is regarded as optional and it is willing to adapt itself to circumstances.

Chapter Four

A Religion Without Christianity: Monasticism

"St. Athanasius, in exile in the capital [Rome], in 341, made monasticism
known there, which, until then, had been despised as a vile and ignominious
thing. And he had also taught there the discipline of virginity."

—R. P. Camelot, in *Vie spirituelle*,
July 1949, p. 7, citing from St. Jerome, *P.L.* 5, 1089–90.

MODERN MAN REJECTS "THE RELIGIOUS LIFE" BECAUSE IT IS a principle of separation in a humanity which is already too cruelly divided. Earlier eras prized titles, rank, uniforms, and habits that identified one as belonging to a privileged class. But our age rejects and abandons such things. Priests wear suits, and even soldiers (when they can) wear civilian clothes. Today, we want to be men—nothing more, and nothing less.

Christians, too, want to be men like other men. They want to participate fully with other men, and on terms of equality. And they want to do so because Christ has taught us that the whole of human existence, and not only its margins and its pastimes, must be filled with meaning, with value, with creative love.

The basic contemporary concept, which explains atheism, secularization, and the crisis of the Church and of faith, is that there are not two worlds and two lives of which man must choose one. There is a single life and a single world, and this life and this world must be lived totally. This concept, as we have seen, is opposed to that of "religion." And, along with the hierarchy, the greatest factor in the transformation of Christianity into a religion is monasticism, or the religious life.

The establishment of a priestly caste in the early centuries of the Church robbed the faithful of their dignity, of their liberty as "priests," "kings," and "prophets." But the appearance, in the fourth century, of hermits and cenobites completed their "reduction to the lay state."

Although, according to the New Testament, all Christians were "spiritual men" since they had received the Spirit, and all belonged to the people of God (*laos*), and all belonged to the clergy because all had a share in the Word of God and in salvation (see Küng, *The Church*, pp. 512–35), a distinction—a sacrilege, in the proper sense of the term—was now introduced between spiritual men and carnal men, between religious and secular men, between "states of perfection" and "states of imperfection," between those who were proprietors of the Beatitudes and those who had to resign themselves to being third-class Christians.

The monks, despite their truly admirable virtues and the large number of saints who peopled their cloisters, developed a spirituality of escape. Their idealism, their otherworldliness, created, by way of reaction, the spirit of materialism and atheism that characterizes so many contemporary movements. The monks abandoned the world for God. The laity, therefore, concluded that, if one were to give oneself to the world, one must abandon God. The tragic part of this is that the true God, the Christian God, was obviously ignored as much by one side as by the other. For this was the God that had so loved the world that he sent his Son, his *sons*, into the world to save the world.

In order to study the progressive paganization of Christianity, we will consider successively asceticism, monasticism, and eschatology.

1. *Asceticism*

By asceticism I do not mean only the self-discipline that is necessary for everyone to acquire mastery over himself, but especially the practice peculiar to "religious" by virtue of which they voluntarily deprive themselves of certain pleasures and certain goods in order to find for themselves a more direct access to God. Celibacy, which is so widely discussed today, is a typical example of asceticism.

An expert on the subject has this to say: "It is known that asceticism is the road to power. An individual remains voluntarily under his legal and material potential. . . . He thus maintains a certain margin, always increasing, between what he could do, legally and practically, and what he actually is content to do. Each act of renouncement, in this mysterious world, is entered on the credit side of the ledger, and assures one of a corresponding margin of supernatural potential. One thus acquires, in the world of the impossible and the forbidden, a hereafter which is reserved to himself alone and which corresponds exactly to what has been renounced in the world of the possible and the allowed. This is an exceedingly advantageous exchange, for what one renounces in the realm of the profane is obtained in that of the sacred. In this way, the ascetic increases his powers to the extent that he decreases his pleasures, separates himself from men, draws near to the gods, and soon becomes their rival. This imbalance is now to the advantage of the ascetic, and the gods, regretting the necessity of having to pay a fair price for so much self-maceration, will lead the ascetic into all sorts of temptations in order to make him lose the power that threatens to make him their equal. This theme is common in all mythologies."[1] Needless to say, it is also easy to find in the lives of the Fathers of the Desert.

Asceticism, in the sense described above, is deeply pagan. It represents man's effort *par excellence* to acquire power over God. Christianity recognizes and even requires renunciation; but it requires it of everyone, and not as a prerequisite of power but as a condition of love and of service. "You cannot be the slave both of God and of money" (Matthew 6:24), and "none of you can be my disciple unless he gives up all his possessions" (Luke 14:33).

Christian mortification is not, as it was long believed (through a misunderstanding that both narrowed its meaning and broadened its application), an optional invitation to make one's body suffer. Rather, it is a general obligation to *destroy* one's evil passions. ("That is why you must kill everything in you that belongs only to earthly life: fornication, impurity, guilty passion, evil desires and especially greed, which is the same thing as worshiping a false god" [Colossians 3:5]). It is not from the body, but from the heart that these things come; and it is not the body, but the heart that must be mortified (see Matthew 15:19).

This is something very different from an asceticism that makes one deprive oneself of what is allowed (sleep, marriage, food); that seeks to frustrate man's most legitimate desires; that cultivates suffering needlessly; that col-

[1] Roland Caillois, *L'Homme et le sacré*, p. 29.

lects acts of poverty, of obedience, and of virginity, and yet forgets the great commandment of brotherly love. The difference between this kind of asceticism and that ordered in the Gospel is that the latter has meaning only when it is undertaken in the service of love, and has no meaning when it is pursued for its own sake.

The New Testament represents a strong reaction against asceticism. It praises the sinner who accepts God's grace in his indignity, and it blames the Pharisee who refuses God's gift and refuses to believe that he has need of God's pardon. John the Baptist and his followers practiced rigorous fasts and a spectacular asceticism. "For John the Baptist comes, not eating bread nor drinking wine. . . ." Jesus practiced no asceticism, but acted with a freedom becoming to a son of God: "The Son of Man comes, eating and drinking, and you say, 'Look, a glutton and a drunkard'" (Luke 7:33–34). Jesus freed his followers from the traditional practices of natural religion by forbidding them to put his new wine in old wineskins. He exhorted his disciples to watch and pray, but never to fast. (The two places in the Gospel that speak of fasting are interpolations and do not appear in the Jerusalem Bible (Mark 9:29, Matthew 17:21). These interpolations are frequently cited, however, and reveal how thoroughly the Church was re-Judaicized after the initial explosion of evangelical freedom.)

For Jesus, "the bridegrooms attendants would never think of fasting while the bridegroom is still with them" (Mark 2:19). And who would dare assert that we have lost the Bridegroom, that the Church is a widow, and that we are orphans? When Jesus says, "The time will come for the bridegroom to be taken away from them, and then, on that day, they will fast" (2:20), he is predicting his death, when the bereaved apostles will once more fall under the yoke of Jewish law because of their lack of faith. But, after the Resurrection, the Bridegroom will be given back to them, and, with him, freedom.

Jesus' fast in the desert symbolizes his identification with Israel, and it is no more to be taken literally than is the flight into Egypt. One must no more look for a basis for fasting in the first instance than for an exhortation to pilgrimage in the second. Fasts, vigils, celibacy, flagellations—these are all human means that have no "sacred" efficacy with respect to our relations with God. Whether one is married or single, the only way to God is through love.

The cross that we are all invited to bear is the one that must inevitably come if we fight for justice, if we trust men, if we allow ourselves to be inspired by the love that led Jesus to Calvary. But no one orders us to go out and look for that cross. The ascetic who wants to suffer in order to resemble Christ unconsciously separates himself from Christ. The Passion of Jesus was not an exercise in asceticism, a calculated mortification, a voluntary mutilation. It was simply an act of love. Christ did not waste his time seeking out ways to suffer. He did not stop thinking about the Father and about his mission so as to have more time to think about himself. He sought the will of his Father, he gave himself over entirely to men; and that is what led him to the cross. The cross of Christ, therefore, cannot be sought in our little personal acts of asceticism; it must result from our love of the Father and of men.

St. Paul also reacted against human means of assuring salvation. Asceticism was, for him, a "work of the flesh." He says: "It may be argued that true wisdom is to be found in these, with their self-imposed devotions, their self-abasement, and their severe treatment of the body; but once the flesh starts to protest, they are no use at all" (Colossians 2:23).

The Council of Jerusalem dispensed Christians from following Jewish law; but this law was too natural, too much in keeping with man's old religious sentiments, not to reappear quickly. Man is always strongly tempted to work out his salvation for himself, independently of God and of other men. Apparently, the only form of self-discipline that frightens the ascetic is that of associating with his fellow men.

The ignorance of the monks, and the influence of neo-Platonism, combined to obliterate the distinction between "the battle against the flesh" (which, in the New Testament, signifies the "old man"—i.e., the man opposed to God), and maceration of the flesh. This confusion was the source of the ascetic performances of the Fathers of the Desert, of the "penances" that ruined the health of St. Bernard and of so many others, and of the "reformation" of the Trappists by Father Jean-Armand de Rancé.

Authentic Christian spirituality is aware that excessive fasting makes one as incapable of service as does excessive eating. What is necessary, in either case, is that the spirit be free and available for the service of God and one's brothers. Or, even better, one may make abstinence from alcohol not a laborious and depressing exercise, but a condition for and a consequence of one's apostolate and of brotherly love. Nothing ensures sobriety so much as loving the poor and sharing what one has with them. The apostles tried on one occasion to make Jesus eat as they did, but he had forgotten his hunger and fatigue in talking to the Samaritan woman. He was excited at having been able to confide in her as in no one before, and he answered, "I have food that you do not know about. . . . My food is to do the will of the one who sent me" (John 4:34). Ascetics choose to imitate Jesus' refusal of food, but not his enthusiasm for the apostolate. There are monks, for example, who are not allowed to speak to women.

To sum up, we must say that Christianity is not a renunciation, but an expression of preference. Christianity reveals someone to us who dispenses us from being rich or gluttonous; it shows us a treasure for which we are willing to give up everything else. The true cross of the Christian is his brother, but it is first of all his love. This is the asceticism of the Gospel, and it is the asceticism that is proper for our time.

2. Monasticism

The true "monk" is the hermit (the cenobites do in groups what the hermit does alone). And the word "hermit" tells us all that we need to know.

Vast reserves of intelligence have been expended vainly in attempts to explain how the elite of Christianity, whose greatest commandment is love and service of one's neighbor, came to believe that perfection consists in flight from one's neighbor. Christ created a Church in order to save men; and the monks decided to save themselves by running away from that Church. Jesus entered into the history of men; but some of his disciples decided that it was better to escape from men and look for God in the desert. St. Paul (Romans 9:3) would have been willing to be separated from Christ if it meant that he would be able to save his brothers; the monks decided to abandon their brothers in order to be united to God. In monasticism, the two principal means of spiritual perfection are those about which Christ said not a word: contemplation, and the cloister.

One would have to take literally what Jesus said about Satan's being the "Prince of this world," or what St. Paul called the "spirit of the world" to find a justification for withdrawing from the world—and especially for ignoring Jesus' explicit words: "I am not asking you to remove them [his followers] from the world, but to protect them from the evil one. . . . As you have sent me into the world, I have sent them into the world" (John 17:15-18). Indeed, although one may look for justification in the Bible, the ascetics were actually giving in to their natural religiosity and succumbing to the influences of pagan asceticism and of neo-Platonic spiritualism.

The way in which monasticism succeeded in perverting Christianity was in causing it to give up the struggle to sanctify daily life. For monks, salvation can be found only in a "special" way, by means of a spiritual quest reserved to a few men.[2] And yet, the essence of Revelation lies in

[2] For a long time, "monastic profession [i.e., the vows] were considered by the Church as a practically indispensable means of attaining Christian perfection rapidly." René Voillaume, *Au coeur des masses,* Paris, Editions du Cerf, 2nd ed., p. 186.

the proclamation of a Kingdom that is open to all, to the poor, the humble, to the ignorant, to sinners—and not only to "specialists" and to those who are "perfect." The sign that we had passed from death to life is this, that we love our brothers. But the hermit deserted his brother, abandoned his political, economic, social, and even his apostolic responsibilities to devote himself to his own "spiritual life."

This is the cause of the present crisis. Because spirituality was so long cultivated apart from life, men had to learn to live without spirituality. A catastrophic division was created between nonbelievers, who wish to give the greatest possible meaning to human life through political, economic, and social action, and believers, who look for that meaning exclusively, or at least chiefly, in "religion" and the "spiritual."[3]

[3] Here are the words of Pius XI in praise of the Trappists and Christians who renounce the active apostolate and vow themselves perpetually and exclusively to prayer and penance: "Those who diligently pursue the office of prayer and penance contribute, even more than those who work in the field of the Lord, to the progress of the Church and the salvation of the human race, for, if they did not cause an abundance of divine grace to come down from heaven to water that field, the evangelical workers would harvest a meager crop for all of their efforts." *Umbratilem*, bull of July 8, 1924.

These words assume that apostolic work is neither a prayer nor a sacrifice, and that the prayers of the contemplative monk excuse him from work. Is there a spiritual efficacy superior to that of an apostolate lived in the spirit of love?

And, even in attempting to justify contemplatives on the basis of their invisible fruitfulness, are we not appraising them from a point of view that they themselves reject. After all, they give up the world to devote themselves to God—and we congratulate them for serving the world. The truth of the matter is that, if God can be attained in a more direct way than by loving our brothers as Jesus loved them, then that way can be justified—as long as we realize that it serves no one but the individual who makes use of it.

The essential significance of the Council is that it represented a reaction intended to reconcile Christianity and the world, to declericalize the Church, and to proclaim the spiritual validity of the active life. The most perfect asceticism for Christians is not abstinence or fasting, but the struggle for justice and freedom. The best worship that can be offered to God is not a ceremony, but a life of service and love.

We must recognize, of course, that contemplative, ascetic, and mystical experiences have created men of singular value. But it is equally true that action-oriented spirituality has created even more superior men. If the great commandment of Christianity is brotherly love, then that commandment can better be obeyed in a life of action, of creation, of collaboration, than in one devoted entirely and exclusively to isolation, meditation, and the liturgy.

We are justified in blaming monasticism for having taught and practiced the erroneous doctrine that we must eliminate human relations and renounce the full use of our faculties in order to develop our relations with God. We can reproach them for having preached that certain religious exercises (solitude, celibacy, obedience, fasting) are more effective means of being united to God than a life of brotherly love.

This spiritual perversion has never been condemned. But, as it evolved in a Christian world, it began almost of itself to abandon its own ideals. The hermits were replaced by the cenobites; the cenobites by the friars and the Jesuits, who gave up the office in choir and the cloister for the active apostolate. Then there appeared the secular institutes, whose members remained "in the world." And today we hear talk about religious orders of married people. Soon, the "religious" will be completely laicized, and the layman will be fully Christian. Then we will understand that, if it is good to group together believers (and nonbelievers) in order to work in the world, all such distinctions are secondary and temporary. And at that time, Christianity will have succeeded in its religious revolution. It will have created worshipers, not in isolated places or in classes or in particular states of life, but everywhere and in all time, in spirit and in truth.

Gandhi wrote: "When we dip our hands into a basin of water, when we light a fire with a bamboo kindling, when we add up interminable columns of figures in our offices, when we are burned by the sun, when we sink into the mud of the swamps, when we stand before the furnace in a foundry—if, at those moments, we are not living exactly the same religious life as we would if we were at prayer in a monastery, then the world will never be saved."

There is a striking similarity between these words and those of the counciliar text quoted earlier: "All their activities, their prayers and their apostolic undertakings, their conjugal and family life, their recreation of mind and body, if they are lived in the Holy Spirit—and also the trials of life, if they are patiently accepted—all these things become 'spiritual sacrifices, which Jesus Christ has made acceptable to God' (I Peter 2:5)."

Isn't this exactly what Jesus taught and lived in his work as a carpenter and as an apostle?

3. *Eschatology* (*the Doctrine on the End of the World and of Man*)

The monks abandoned secular life because they believed that there was a special sanctifying value in the pagan religious practices of solitude, contemplation, fasting, and self-maceration. Christ has freed Christians from these things by teaching that there is nothing in them to lead us to intimacy with God, and that only fraternal love can create such intimacy—fraternal love lived in the whole of one's existence (of which the sacraments, correctly celebrated, are the signs and sources, or the "commemoration"). The present-day process of secularization has reestablished "the sanctifying value of those 'nonreligious' activities that form the essential part of the day of the faithful as a whole."[4]

And so, the monks, seeing the validity of their life questioned in this world, are now taking refuge in another world. They have announced that the monastic life is a prefiguration of the condition of those who will rise from the dead; that they are now living in the state to which death will one day lead us all. In other words, monastic celibacy, poverty (in a relative sense), and isolation from the world in order to consecrate oneself to God alone allow us to anticipate what the heavenly Jerusalem will be like.

This is a somewhat astonishing claim, not only because "to anticipate" is a convenient way of getting out of

[4] Thils, Gustave, *Christianisme sans religion?*, Paris, Casterman, 1968, p. 148.

having to build, but also and principally because we know absolutely nothing about how we will live our eternity. Eternity is utterly beyond our imagination. It is as silly for us to want to behave now as we will when we are "glorified" as it is for an embryo to want to anticipate its life after birth.

Christ did refer, of course, to a resurrection in which there would be "no marriage or giving in marriage"—which obviously means that there will be no procreation. (Procreation, unfortunately, was long regarded as the only justification for marriage; obviously it would be useless in the afterlife.) But there is no reason for believing that glorification will exclude the continuation of love and friendship.

Revelation speaks to us of the other world through images, and we have no inkling of what those images correspond to. There are banquets, thrones, weddings, and a drinking of new wine. If we want to interpret the words "no marriage or giving in marriage" in a literal sense, then why not do the same for "thrones" and new "wine"?

There are three main schools of theological thought concerning the afterlife. One school believes that heaven is a state of ecstasy. We will be caught up, ravished, immobilized by the eternal and face-to-face contemplation of God. But ecstasy is a paralysis of human faculties —a weakness of which the saints were always wary, and from which Christ never suffered. Christ was more united to God than we will ever be, and this did not prevent the development of his human nature. On the contrary, there is no opposition between our humanity and our divinization. For that matter, what is the use of a "resurrection of the body" if the body is going to lose its faculties immediately? And how could there then be the human effort and the glorification of the cosmos of which St. Paul speaks?

Another school of theologians pictures heaven to be something like the Apocalypse, or like a magnificent monastic celebration, or a liturgical ceremony. But Christianity is opposed to a ritualistic concept of itself. Christianity is not, first and foremost, the liturgy; it is our daily existence, sanctified and sanctifying, and therefore it is that daily existence that must be eternalized and glorified.

More modern theologians, out of respect for earthly reality, like to think of heaven as a world of fraternal communion and creative freedom. *Gaudium et spes* tells us that "the values of dignity, fraternal communion and freedom, all those excellent fruits of our nature and our activity . . . will be recovered."

❀   ❀   ❀

One of the most important questions of our time is: What meaning is there in human activity, and what promises are there for the future?

The eschatologists, who have forsaken technology, science, art, and politics, declare that none of these things are important to salvation. Yves Congar says, "From a purely eschatological and monastic viewpoint, the less we will keep of the world the better it will be. The less time we give to the body and to earthly activities, the better.

Monasticism, in its primitive sense, is a total absence of the world."[5]

We know, however, that a purely spiritual salvation is inconceivable. There can be no redemption of mankind without a technological, economic, social, political, and artistic liberation. All truly human progress is necessarily spiritual progress, for there is no authentic human progress unless there is also progress in justice and in respect and love of man. If by "spiritual" we mean commitment and redemption, then we must say that nothing is more temporal than the spiritual; if God is love, nothing is more human than the divine; if the supernatural is our true destiny, nothing is more natural than the supernatural. For we love one another with the same love that God has for us.

Another theologian, Fr. Leopold Malevez, says: "The idea that the Incarnation of the Son has an impact not only in the spiritual world but also in that of matter is found among ecclesiastical authors . . . The contemporary mastery of matter, political organization, art, philosophy and technology complete Christ and, in completing him, glorify him. . . . Catholicism accepts human progress in every direction as a condition of, and even as a constitutive element in its own perfection.[6] And Yves de Montcheuil, the French Jesuit put to death by the Nazis in 1944, adds that ". . . nothing [other than Christianity] gives such breadth to history . . . by seeing in it the future of the whole Christ."[7]

[5] *Jalons pour une théologie du laïcat*, Paris, Editions du Cerf, 1953, p. 581.
[6] *Révue de théologie*, 1937, pp. 377ff.
[7] *Leçons sur le Christ*, p. 25.

The monks answer that they serve the world by constituting, in the midst of a world which is tempted to regard itself as self-sufficient and to lose itself in pleasure, a reminder of its mortality. Is it really necessary to go to extremes, to exaggerate the reaction to put us on our guard against the danger? It would seem that a true Christian service would be to guide men rather than to frighten them; to teach men to use possessions rather than to reject them. The best travel guides are not people who refuse to travel. Because some men say that man can be saved without God's grace, must the monks proclaim that man can be saved only by God's grace, without human activity?

This point is of some importance, for it is actually a debate between a future life and life eternal. The eschatological monk is waiting for another world, a future life, and he copies the form that he imagines that life will take: contempt for the body and for terrestrial realities. The Christian, on the other hand, believes in life eternal. For him, what is best in this life will be eternalized: the faith and love that he has exercised in his human relations, and the creations that those relations inspire in him. Everything can be sanctified; and thus, in a certain sense, everything can be eternalized. But we do not try to imagine the way in which these will be done; we are content to live the reality of it as profoundly as we can.

Eschatology in its true sense does not focus on life beyond the tomb, but signifies the transcendence, the divine dimension of daily life when it is lived in the Spirit. The tension of Christian life is not between an (imaginary) future life and the future, but between divine life, historically presented, and our tendencies to selfishness, to inertia and despair which are in constant opposition to our higher aspirations.

For centuries, alchemists searched for the philosopher's stone. And for centuries, religions mystified the people by pretending that they had holiness stored away in containers, like patent medicines (sacraments, prayers), or by teaching a shortcut to God (celibacy, contemplation, voluntary suffering) that exempted us from the terrestrial struggle. Christianity, however, pushes us into the midst of this struggle, tells us that we must find in it both our sanctification and the salvation of the world—and tells us that we cannot separate these two things from one another. If the world is to end, it will end not because we wait for it to happen, but because we work for it to happen. We must not anticipate this event by evading it, but hasten it by our activity. We know the date of the end of the world. Mark (13:10) and Matthew (24:14) tell us what it is, and reveal to us our eschatalogical responsibility: "This Good News of the kingdom will be proclaimed to the whole world as a witness to all the nations. And then the end will come."

Man must not "look to the heavens"; he must work on earth. Like the apostles at the Ascension, and like Jonas after his three-day "closed retreat" in the whale's belly, we are pushed out into the world to begin our task.

The Apocalypse of the Jews is oriented toward the future, but the authentic eschatology of Christianity focuses on the decisive nature of the present. The present is of infinite importance because Christ is already here among us, and we have only to discover him.

The image that monastic eschatology has drawn for itself of the end of the world is as simplistic as that of the nineteenth-century Church on the origin of the world. The Church believed in the instantaneous creation of the world as we know it; and then she had to admit, painful as it was, that it had actually resulted from uncounted millions of years of evolution. In the same way, we now believe that the end of the world will not come as the result of an arbitrary decision on God's part, but in consequence of a ripening process for which we are responsible. Teilhard de Chardin, for one, foresaw that the historical completion of human evolution and the final coming of Christ would coincide.

* * *

The conclusion that we may draw from the above reflections is that the monks, by attempting to give their life a maximum of meaning through exclusively spiritual means, achieved admirable results and created men of exceptional quality. The question is now whether we can improve on that experience and give both a human and a divine meaning to life by technical, economic, social, and political research in the full meaning of the term. That is, can we achieve freedom from servitude, establish justice, live in love and respect for man—all under the inspiration of the Spirit of God? Can we unify our lives in such a way as to justify those who refuse to abandon their temporal responsibilities and wish to make use of all of their active and creative faculties?

No one yet knows the answer to those questions. Only the new saints will be able to tell us.

✳   ✳   ✳

One more question remains: Will the world ever end? At a subjective level, it will certainly end for us individually when we die; and even if man succeeds some day in conquering death, it will have ended for those who died previously. Will those who rise from the dead have any relations with the world that they and God loved so much? What object or goal will they have that will be proportionate to their human faculties? God, no doubt. But why not God such as they learned to know him and to reveal him on earth? "Whoever loves is born of God and knows God."

The only thing in man that corresponds to the infinite perfection of God is the limitless perfectibility of creatures. It is useless for the theologians to promise us a beatific vision when we will be perfectly happy in the tranquil possession of the Supreme Good. What the theologians offer is, in fact, rather frightening. For a finite creature, there is nothing worse than a static heaven; and for an imperfect creature (no one even pretends that we will become perfect), what could be worse than to be immobilized in his imperfection? Our active, creative, and communicative faculties cannot remain unemployed. And therefore our celestial happiness must be a human happiness.

> "The walls of Jerusalem had to come tumbling down so that monotheism could spread. The walls of the

Catholic Church must disappear so
that the good news may reach those
for whom it is intended, the totality
of society without distinction. The
sermon on the mount was addressed
to the whole world. When the great
cathedrals were still new, they were
the meeting halls of the public, the
people's theaters. But today, can we
not say that the churches of the
Catholics have become bushel baskets
hiding the light? If so, let them be
removed. Let the churches in which
Christ is held prisoner be opened.
Let them disappear, so that the
earthly city may have its public
places again. Let us build a center
of spiritual research, a meeting place
for men of good will in search of the
meaning of life. Let the searchers
after truth, the men of science, art,
and politics assemble there. Let us
build a spiritual city of the ideas,
aspirations, materials, technologies,
and art of our time. And let the
inhabitants of that city meet together
in God's love."

—Inscription at the entrance to
the Salon d'Art Sacré, Paris

Chapter Five

The Church in the
Service of the World

VATICAN II INITIATED AN UNPRECEDENTED REVOLUTION IN
THE Church. Even the Protestant Reformation seems tame
in comparison. Of course, up to now, it has been an
exclusively theoretical revolution, one that it will probably take more than a century to implement and realize
in all its implications. It will be slowed, and it will be
distracted by superficial reforms. But it is so necessary to
the vitality of the Church, so much more in keeping with
the Gospel than egocentric conservatism and laziness, so
keenly required by the evolution of the world, that nothing will be able to stop it.

This revolution can be summed up in three points:

1. The Church was deeply divided into two classes: a
clergy who held all authority, and a laity so passive that
the hierarchy spoke for practically all the faithful and
acted in their place. This situation has now been reversed.
The Church has rediscovered the priesthood of the laity,
and she now defines herself as the people of God for the
service of whom all ministries have been instituted.

2. For three centuries, the Church was overly occupied
with defending itself against "modern ideas" and with
withdrawing into itself like a fortress under siege. Catholics were required to present a united front in order to
guard the rights of the Church. But today, the Church is
opening itself up with understanding to the world that
she so recently anathematized, and declaring that she
wishes to serve it. The ideas of the French Revolution
were once condemned as coming from the devil, just as

communism was later condemned as "intrinsically perverse"; and yet, those ideas are now celebrated as a realization of the Christian ideal and of Biblical inspiration.[1]

3. The Church once reserved to itself exclusively the benefits of the Redemption; and now it recognizes that one can be saved even if he has never heard of the Church and even if he does not believe in Christ or in God. It regards other religions, and even atheists, as brothers, as holders of truths and of grace, as being called to salvation. It has stopped condemning them, and it has entered into dialogue with them without attempting to proselytize them.

The consequences of these changes are incalculable; and one of the most obvious of these consequences is that the composition of the Church will now change drastically. The partisans of the revolutionary movement have left the Church in great numbers, and are leaving it still. Those who want nothing of importance to be changed, and who regard the Church's majestic immobility as the best reason for faith and as a matter of great pride, are also threatening to leave. The Church vainly attempts to hold back and slow down the progressives in order to avoid losing the conservatives; and, as a result, everyone is dissatisfied. One thing excludes the other. The Church must now choose. She must either remain the prisoner of Catholics who use her as a means of maintaining their privileges, confirming their prejudices and satisfying their own religious needs, but who refuse to listen to her as

[1] See P. Comblin, *Théologie de la révolution,* Editions Universitaires, Paris, 1970, pp. 247–77.

soon as she says anything that contradicts their radical conservatism. Or, she must choose to side with the Christians in the underground churches, with the small informal groups that have no connection with the mother Church but are unwilling to leave her entirely, and which have never given up the hope that they will one day be recognized by the Church as containing that which is best in her.

A decisive factor in the Church's decision must be the existence, between those two opposing groups, of a multitude of simple, poor uninformed people who have neither the motivation of the conservatives for remaining in the Church nor the incentives of the progressives for leaving it and innovating. This mass of people suffer from the discrepancy that they sense between the Church as it is, and the Church that they need. They would be much more comfortable in a renovated Church than in one whose traditional teaching underestimates them and whose requirements do not employ them to their full potential. As soon as these people are addressed in a language that is at once evangelical and modern, as soon as they are freed from outdated concepts and taboos (sacralization of ritual, of priests, of authority, of the Law), as soon as they are shown the true Church, they will enter onto a stage of active Christianity, and they will bring to the Church all the qualities of uprightness, simplicity, generosity, and freshness which they have preserved during their long and patient wait.

It is only with such people that the Church will be able to undertake the prodigious transformation required of it by the Council.

The Great Failure of the Catholic Missions

We occidentals have been raised in the conviction that our Christian civilization is incontestably superior to any other. We possess the truth. We have the true God and the true faith, and our impulses of generosity were limited to carrying these things to other peoples and sharing them with them. Nothing was lacking for the Church to be one, holy, and catholic. She was infallible, and she was without sin since she was, in a sense, the new Incarnation of her Master. "The Church," Bossuet said, "is Jesus Christ, proclaimed and communicated."

We did not realize that, in believing these things, we were identifying Christianity with the West. To become a Christian, so far as we were concerned, meant to become like us. We were unable to think beyond the limits of our own experiences, to conceive of a prayer that did not use our own words and gestures, of worship without our occidental rites, of salvation without "our" Church.

Instead of realizing that our particular brand of Christianity was only one particular way of knowing the message of Jesus, and instead of admitting that that knowledge had been conditioned by a history and a culture peculiar to us and thus inapplicable to others, we attempted to impose it—that is, to impose ourselves—on everyone else.

When I was still young, the Belgian Jesuit missiologist Father Charles had just formulated his celebrated definition of missionary work, a definition that was long regarded as the classical one: "to implant the Church." The purpose of the missions was to create a cell of the Church on foreign territory and thus to extend, fortify, and propagate the sole means of human salvation.

The Church had become, in a sense, an end unto itself. She had convinced herself that she was responding to the (silent) appeal of pagan peoples and bringing them happiness by increasing the number of her faithful. Even when she did not brand non-Christian religions as diabolical superstitions, she held firmly to the belief that her own realization of Christianity was the model of perfection and plenitude that must be adopted by everyone else.

This was the cause of the catastrophic failure of the Catholic missions. Non-Westerners felt that they were neither understood nor respected in their own cultural milieu, in their beliefs, and, above all, in their ability to accept and to interpret truly Christian values. And they were correct. There were no truly native churches in China, Africa, Japan, or India. In an exercise of spiritual imperialism not dissimilar to that practiced by the Western nations at the political and economic level, the Church was more concerned with occidentalizing orientals than in evangelizing them, and in this she was aided by her converts themselves, who proved to be the most determined opponents of a naturalized Christianity. They felt that they would lose caste, and that Christianity itself would be lowered, if their Church were de-Europeanized.

This trend has been reversed by Vatican II. The Church is now the servant. She is no longer an end unto herself. Her purpose is to place herself in the service of the nations so that they may create their own Christianity, starting from the message of Christ. Missionary work now consists in revealing the God who calls everyone to himself and who has always loved all men, to announce to them the good news that the Kingdom of God has arrived among them and that they have received, along with the Gospel, everything that they need to be able to build a Church as good as, or better than, our own.

If the message of Christ is to be truly liberating for all peoples, it must first deliver the Church herself from her human traditions and her unconscious pride. The Churches that will be born and grow under the inspiration of the Holy Spirit and the control of native bishops will be neither less holy nor less orthodox than our Western Church—even if they are less Roman.

Judaism was once the centralizing agent and the focus of true belief. One had to be a Jew in order to enter into the Covenant. There was but one Law, and one temple in which the people could worship. But the prophets announced a universal religion, and they felt free to carry it to the pagans. Jesus himself created an open and centrifugal community which was to be the leaven in the dough and would transform the whole of humanity—not by the imposition of a single Law, but by the inspiration of the Spirit communicated freely to all.

For a long time the Church believed that it was "saving its soul"—i.e., guarding the deposit of the faith and ensuring its unity by means of centralization—in binding the five continents to the philosophy of Aquinas, to the theology of Italy, to the liturgy of Rome, and to the language of a vanished empire. If particularism is unacceptable because it sacrifices unity to the tyranny of one man, uniformity is even worse, because it is nothing more than particularism striving to impose itself on the whole world.

Christ said that only in losing our souls can we hope to save them. In other words, the Gospel will be preached fruitfully only if we are willing to abandon the forms in which we have imprisoned it over the past two thousand years. The Gospel must seem to lose itself in the soil of foreign civilizations before it can spring up, in unimaginable new forms, to provide harvests without number.

The Word of God was first expressed in a Semitic language and in Semitic conceptual categories; it was later defined in Greco-Latin terms. It must now be able to express itself in Indian, Chinese, and African categories. There is an occidental theology, and there is an oriental theology; and the two are very different.

This flexibility of expression is a necessary step in evolution. For someone to be permeated with the faith, the faith must be able to speak to him at every level. It must utilize and modify his intellectual, moral, imaginative, emotional and spiritual structures. And, in doing so, the faith will find new depth and new wealth of expression. "The Church is catholic, not only because she carries salvation and truth to all peoples in all times, but also because she requires the cooperation of all civilizations and all men in order to bring to light the wealth of the deposit that she has received, and to build the eternal city of God."[2]

In order to preserve this "deposit" from corruption, it

[2] Yves de Montcheuil, *Problèmes de vie spirituelle,* p. 63.

is surely not necessary for us to encase it in formulas devised centuries ago—formulas that now mean nothing even to us Westerners. If men are to accept the message of Christ, they will do so, in any case, only to the extent that they perceive that message in their own language and according to their own mentality.

In our attempts to uproot and denationalize our converts, we have made them strangers in their own lands, foreigners among their brothers. We have left them unstable, unsatisfied, ripe for schism and heresy, prone to form sects that promise to fill the void which we have created. Everywhere, people are asking for prophets—for men who cannot believe that Revelation is really a "deposit," that faith is actually a passive acceptance of occidental dogmas, that liturgy is a ceremony independent of the mentality of those who celebrate it.

The people of Israel did not discover the true wealth of their religion in their own land, but among strangers, in exile. They discovered that this wealth did not lie, as they had believed, in their temple, their rites, their priests, their rules, but in their faith—a faith that could flourish even when it had been uprooted, and that could be accepted by the people with whom they lived.

In the same way, the primitive Church discovered the gift of Christ, the liberation of Christ, the unfathomable riches of Christ, only when it fled its Palistinian ghetto. When the apostles and missionaries had been chased out by persecution and forced to flee into pagan lands, then and only then, in contact with nonbelievers, did they discover and develop the doctrine of the universality of the Redemption. And only then did they reject the Jewish categories that had almost succeeded in smothering the new faith.

*   *   *

The question of the Church's missionary activity must be studied today in all its ramifications, for it does not concern only the people of the Third World. It is not only the Africans and the Chinese who feel remote from present-day Catholicism, but also the workers when they see a middle-class Church; the poor, when they see a rich Church; scholars and scientists, when they see a Church that still speaks of dogmas and miracles. Christianity must now prove that it can become truly catholic; and it will be able to do so only if it abandons the claim that it is already catholic. As Hans Küng points out, the catholicity of the Church is not a claim based on pride, but a humble duty. The Church as it exists among us is not the plenitude of other churches and other religions. The only plenitude that it knows is that of Christ, who is working constantly to complete the Church—but who is also working equally to complete the other churches so that "all things may be fulfilled in all men."

Union Among the Churches

The timidity of the official ecumenical movement is a matter of disenchantment to young people and to everyone who, conscious of the urgency of union, realizes that it will never be achieved if it is left in the hands of the theologians and the Vatican diplomats. Under prophetic inspiration, these people want to bypass the authorities by means of such gestures as intercommunion and demonstrations of brotherhood.

This phenomenon reopens a question that seemed to have been solved. Is doctrinal unanimity necessary for union among the churches? If so, then we must be prepared for a long wait indeed!

Is there any real hope that the Catholic Church will one day admit that its dogmas are in need of reformation, or that the other churches will accept those dogmas? The ecumenists make a great to-do about the declaration of Vatican II that "there is an order and a hierarchy of values among Catholic doctrines." But, as we have said before, this is like proclaiming that some doctrines are more infallible than others.

The only true road to union is a doctrinal and disciplinary pluralism. And, with respect to the limits of that pluralism, let us ask ourselves this question: Is the unity that Christ wishes for his disciples a unity of love and faith in his person and his word, or is it merely a union in credos and in theological theses?

We must be very wary of ideas. Ideas must be verified, reinterpreted, renewed constantly. We establish contact with one another at the level of ideas, but we understand one another at the level of experience and of life. What is essential in the life of the different churches is expressed not in their theological debates, but in their common struggle against the same difficulties: against the indifference of the world to their message, against individualism and passivity among the faithful, against clericalism among the pastors, against the inflexibility of their institutions, against inadequate reflection and research, and especially against spiritual lassitude.

Certainly, ideas are important when they are closely tied to the experiences which they express. It is absolutely necessary that we be able to express consciously what we feel. A love and a faith that are not expressed are not human. Theologians (and every Christian must be something of a theologian) must be able to articulate and clarify what they believe, and let us not forget that true charity toward someone who is (we think) in error consists in providing him with patient explanations.

Even so, when it comes to reconciling different expressions of belief, it is far more effective to intensify our experiences than to discuss our formulations. What is important here is that we be able to identify with the Christian experiences of others (even if they are not, for the moment, the same as ours), and that we be able, perhaps definitively, to identify with their interpretation of those experiences. If both parties accept Revelation and are willing to become more and more attentive and faithful to Revelation, surely that is sufficient basis for sincere communication and fruitful collaboration. When a man declares that he does not want to be separated from Jesus Christ, and that he wishes to make his thoughts and his conduct conform more and more to Christ's teaching, it seems highly improbable that he can truly be separated from other men who share the same commitment.

The main cause of division among the churches is not diversity of belief, nor even tension among apparently irreconcilable opinions, but that sense of exclusivity that refuses to love and to exercise patience in order to resolve differences. In the very first generation of Christians there were serious differences in doctrine, discipline, and tactics; but there was sufficient charity, too, to prevent a schism. It was not until much later that schisms could be justified on the basis of quarrels over the date of Easter, over whether the Eucharistic bread must be leavened or unleavened, and over the *Filioque*. One wonders by what spirit the Church was inspired to excommunicate Christians over such matters.

Love is the mortar of union, and orthodoxy is the fruit of it. What makes unity in the Church is not a uniformity of credos, but the *will* to live together, to have the same God, the same Lord, the same faith, the same Gospel. It is not the will to have one's own God, one's own Lord, one's own faith. The *will* to unite creates a real union, even though it may not immediately create agreement on all matters.

If we require that others, to love us, must agree with us, then it is we who do not love our brothers. Instead, we love only ourselves. If we love only that which resembles us, then we do not love at all. What makes a marriage is not an identity of opinions (for then the marriage would break up over the first difference) but a love that enables the couple to overcome their disagreements.

Charity—that is, love—does not abolish disagreement, but surpasses it and envelops it. In the first Council of Jerusalem, for example, no one was condemned, not even the Hellenists or the Judaizers. Instead, an attempt was made to overcome differences of opinion by adopting practical measures that allowed everyone to live together and to communicate. The Church of Jerusalem and the Pauline churches remained united, despite all their quarrels, denunciations, and discussions, not because of dogmatic definitions, but because they had a community of love and a common fund of experiences.

The union of churches today will not be brought about by the debates of theologians, however competent they may be, but by an increase of life and of love. Let Protestants and Catholics become more Christian; and let them both, in turning to Jesus Christ, draw near to one another.

No one has a monopoly on fidelity to Christ. Such fidelity requires a perpetual conversion on the part of every church; and when a church begins to live again and to burn in Christ, she draws all the others toward Christ and toward unity. She brings the other churches to the proper temperature for fusion to occur.

No one is the sole proprietor of truth. No church has a complete inventory of Christ's message. All churches have a long way to go in that respect. Why not then allow one another to make such progress in the bonds of fraternal unity? This sort of brotherhood will bring about a convergence of experiences and expressions rather than the contrary.

One thing is certain, and this is that the road to unity is not that of dogmatic concessions and horse trading. Instead, it is a road that leads everyone to the same place, to a Christ who is better understood and better listened to. It is not a question of sacrificing truth or of putting a stop to research and discussion. In fact, our discussions are prolonged more by the fossilization of dogmas than by an excess of research. The churches are held captive by their dogmas and their structures because they lack resilience; but fresh and living thought, and a historical examination, would set them free again. True fidelity for everyone consists in attaching oneself to the truth in order to examine it, understand it, and renew it, and also in having enough respect for others to believe that, in this climate of love, they will make as much progress as we toward the truth. There is infinitely more respect for truth in this attitude than in demanding that someone deny what he believes is true so as to remain united with us. Indeed, it would be difficult to think of anything more opposed to the spirit of love than this imperious urge to impose on others a truth that we ourselves have taken so long to discover.

On this question, there is a reform that the Church's recently acquired respect for the individual conscience makes absolutely indispensable for the Catholic in his profession of faith. Up until now, the Church has required that Catholics accept every one of the articles of the Credo. Anyone who did not accept one dogma was considered to reject them all. The pretext for this was the belief that, if a Catholic could not accept even a single point, he was rejecting the "formal motive" of the Credo, which was faith in the Word of God as proclaimed by the Church.

This attitude makes adherence to truth a matter of discipline rather than of conviction, and it serves only to exclude many conscientious Christians from the Church.

How can one assent to a truth that is not perceived as a truth, or that perhaps has no meaning for the individual, simply because it is dictated by someone in whom one is supposed to have confidence? In so delicate a matter, we should be careful to make the proper distinctions between "assent," "nonrejection," and "suspension of judgment."

The fact of the evolution of dogma demonstrates quite well that the search for understanding of the faith requires time, perseverance, and respect for the work of the Holy Spirit. In the thirteenth century, St. Thomas Aquinas denied the Immaculate Conception; and yet he is not excommunicated. Why, then, should we not admit in space what we admit in time? If the Protestants—or a Catholic, for that matter—are of the same opinion as St. Thomas, why should we not allow them sufficient time for evolution? Why is it that we do not excommunicate Thomas, but excommunicate those who hold the same opinion as he? "Because," someone will say, "the Church has defined that dogma since the time of Aquinas." And that, of course, is the whole problem. Should the Church, in fact, ever define a dogma in an authoritarian and exclusive manner? If the Church needs nineteen centuries to be able to discern a dogma in Revelation, why should she not allow other Christians to take a few extra centuries, more or less? And, while we are waiting, we can ask them not to condemn us for our faith in the Immaculate Conception, just as *we* do not condemn *them* for refusing to believe in it. In this way, dialogue could go on, even though we might not ever reach an agreement. The Protestants would agree to study the question further, while we would try to marshal more persuasive arguments and more precise explanations for our thesis.

It is possible that some Protestants—and some non-Thomist Catholics—do not accept the doctrine of transubstantiation. But this does not make intercommunion impossible, as long as they believe in the presence of Christ at the Last Supper. In any case, it would be better for us to find another formula for this dogma, one on which an agreement would be possible.

Surely, the Christian churches have enough in common to enable them to bear with one another's differences. So long as we all assent to Revelation and to Jesus Christ, why must we disobey our founder in such a scandalous manner for the pure joy of making subtle and secondary distinctions?

To excommunicate someone who does not agree with us hardly seems the best method of convincing him that he is wrong. There must be authority in the Church, of course; but that authority must be exercised in a Christian, and not in an imperial, manner. Excommunication is the equivalent of banishment, and can we banish someone from salvation? We can tell him that, in the opinion of the Church as a whole, he has wandered from the path of truth; but this is a far cry from cutting him off from our love. If the unity of the Church has been ruptured, it is because those who exercise authority have used their office as a "power" rather than as a "service of communion."

To sum up, it seems that the Church went wrong when she made full adherence to her dogmas a condition of participation in her life. One ceases to be a Christian

only when one refuses the Gospel; that is, when one refuses to believe in Jesus and to love one's brothers in
spite of all obstacles. One does not cease to be a Christian
because one cannot believe such and such a dogma. If
Protestants find inadmissible our explanation of Christ
in the Eucharist by transubstantiation, but if they wish
nonetheless to take part in our Masses out of fidelity to
Christ, surely we must, rather than refuse to admit them,
affirm our faith in them by living it so well that it becomes
contagious.

It is difficult to understand why we insist on raising
such irritating questions as that of the validity of the
Protestant ministry. We must have a very strange and
narrow notion of the apostolate if we really believe that
God would deny ministers to the Protestants because, in
our view, several centuries ago there was an interruption
in the apostolic succession of their bishops, or some ir-
regularity in their ceremony of ordination. Grace, after
all, is not transmitted like an electrical current. The Catholic Church recognizes that it is possible to "supply" grace
when her own system breaks down. Why cannot we admit
the same thing for other systems?

*   *   *

I will be happy if I never hear again the solemn words,
"God will reunite us when he wishes and in the manner
that he wishes." Such formalistic repetitions are too easily
used to justify negligence and hypocrisy. We can be sure
that God wants us to be reunited, and that he wants it to
happen immediately. The only obstacle to this reunion is
ourselves. If we wait for God to effect reunion, we will
have to wait forever. God has already done his part

through the love which he offers and the call that he addresses to us. All that we have to do is answer. It is we, after all, who divided the churches; and it is up to us to reunite them—immediately.

It is possible for the union of churches to take place now. But, unless we are willing to go about it in using a new approach, it will never take place. God will judge us on our love, and not on our faith. The churches can perfect their Credos and their liturgies as much as they wish; and they will still be condemned by their inability to unite, their lack of warmth and vitality, and their poverty in love.

One day, as the Holy Days approached, Jesus assembled the people, not in the temple but in the desert, and celebrated the feast by a great sharing of bread. If the churches would do the same thing; if only once, at Easter, they would abandon their splendid and vain ceremonies and replace their "worship" by a universal sharing of bread, they would be able immediately to unite, and then they would be in a position to unite the world in a liturgy that would be, finally, meaningful.

The Church and the World—and the Third World

The union of the churches, as urgent as it is, is only secondary. As Robinson says, the reconciliation of the churches, if it takes place, will probably be a marriage of senior citizens. In other words, the churches will by then have become completely useless, and will have to unite in order to combine their vanishing flocks.

Behind the idea of unity is another, more important, idea. Is Christianity capable of uniting the world, of helping all religions and all knowledge to go beyond themselves in the recognition of a universal value?

Christianity, at its origin, was a powerful movement of liberation and of respect for man. But it has now become a bastion of conversation and oppression. Of course, we could put the original pieces back together again; but that would not bring the Church back to life. It will live again, and will begin to have an impact on the world again, only if it regenerates itself. At the present time, in all its forms, the Church suffers from a terrible lack of spiritual vitality and of attraction for men. Its immense administrative organism and its ponderous structures, far from creating life, are only wasting the little energy that remains. The Church, to put it brutally, repels as much as the Gospel attracts.

The first service that the Church owes to the world, therefore, is to become once more a place of love and of action, a community of the saved, a manifestation of the Spirit, a celebration of the creative gift of God.

In a society such as that of the contemporary world, in which there is no meditation, no prayer, no communion, no interior freedom, and no God—in which innumerable "poor" people have been forced, by the void in their lives, to take their opium straight, without religion —there is an immense, although still unconscious, spiritual need. But once these people become aware that there are witnesses to God, masters of the spiritual life, fervent communities, centers where the Word and the Bread are shared, we will be astonished at the intensity and scope of the resulting Christian renaissance. And we are not talking only about the interior life of the Church. The Church is weighted down by the burden of its past and by her withdrawal into herself. She must now open herself up to the future, strip herself of everything except the Gospel, so that she may receive the inspiration of the One who renews incessantly the face of the world and of the Church.

✻   ✻   ✻

What must the Church do in order to become once more a source of hope among the people? The answer is simple enough. She must become Christian again. She must rediscover her basic message, the message of freedom from the Law, from sin, from death, from everything that prevents man from living; the message of respect for, and service of, man; the message of faith in an unlimited future that we must create together.

For the first time in history, it seems, men of every continent are becoming aware of their vocation as men, of their need for freedom and dignity. This great outpouring of hope has been called forth by the Gospel; and it is only the Gospel that can justify and nourish it.

But the Church seems unaware of this phenomenon. She has reestablished the old pagan distinction between our duties to God and our duties to man, and she has allowed herself to become absorbed in the ritual of worship and the exercise of authority. She has become a religion like all the others; and, like all the others, she is incapable of inspiring hope among the people. She is no longer the good news of human liberation, but the bulwark of the established order. When the Pope goes to

Latin America, to Asia, or to Africa, despite the best of intentions, he gives support to his brother chiefs of state rather than hope to the oppressed.

The present disagreement between the men who simply lead and those who go forward, the debate between the partisans of verticalism and those of horizontalism, between the champions of God-without-man and those of man-without-God, are all the absurd consequence of the Church's long-time infidelity to her original inspiration. Jesus united, in himself and for all time, man and God, the horizontal with the vertical. God in Jesus disappeared in man's presence—not to annihilate himself, but to become more alive by becoming that by means of which we love one another.

The Church must discover once more the newness of the Gospel. Only then will her message become once more the message of freedom: everything that is sacred (God, the temple, the rituals) were placed by Jesus in the service of man. Jesus did not make a political, social, or economic revolution; instead, he accomplished a greater revolution, one that would inspire all other revolutions. He revolutionized religion. He desacralized all authority by placing the authority of God himself at the service of man. So far as the Church is concerned, the true worship of God consists in defending man wherever he is oppressed, and in comforting him whenever he is unhappy. The God of the Church is the God who has brought man to life, who has enabled him to rise upward to the extent of his capacity—that is, indefinitely. There are not two worlds, one which belongs to God and the other to man. There is a single world, created, animated, and inspired by God. And the true development of that world is identical with the salvation preached by the churches. It is time to unite once more those who love God and those who love man; and even their combined strength will not be too much in the battle against those who love neither God nor man.

*   *   *

The Church's potential field of action is vast. The social issues of the nineteenth century have become the world issues of the twentieth. It is no longer a class of people, but whole nations and entire continents, who are being oppressed and proletariatized. It is there that the Church must preach the good news and launch an undertaking around which men can rally. Let the Church stop wasting the energy of the faithful in ceremonies and rites, in prayers without action (all ecclesiastical exhortations end with the words "Pray for this" and "Pray for that"), and in "receiving" the sacraments. What is needed today is hope; and it is the task of the Church to raise up a measure of hope that is proportionate to the misery and the frustrations of the poor.

Young people too are looking for a way to do something. They know what is wrong, but there is nothing they can do about it. They revolt against an affluence that alienates, as the poor revolt against their misery. Superficially, youth seems soft and self-centered; but this is only a reaction against society's attempts to break its spirit. Young people can be mobilized—but they can be mobilized in the service of nothing less than a worldwide revolution. It is useless to speak to them of careers and patriotism and religions. They will answer that nothing matters except the Third World, the revolution, social injustice at the national and international levels.

In the nineteenth century the Church deserted the working class. In the twentieth, she is losing the under-developed nations, and, in our own countries, she is being abandoned by the young. But there is still time for her to regain everything that she has lost—if she becomes once more the evangelical crucible of world revolution through her faith in the future of man.

*   *   *

"Repent and do penance for your sins!"

This brief but eloquent declaration, by which John the Baptist, Jesus, and the apostles began their ministries and caught the attention of their generation, today leaves us puzzled and cold. How, we wonder, could anything like that unleash a popular reaction of enthusiasm? The answer is that the words "repent" and "penance" do not refer, as we might think, to self-mortification, fasting, and taking on lugubrious airs, but to a radical change in mentality and orientation. They mean: "Reject your old habits. Take a new direction in your lives. Adopt a new set of values."

We are now in the process of discovering the political implications of that exhortation. It refers not only to individuals, but also to social and national structures. Its true meaning, its least unfaithful translation, is simply: "Revolution!"

We hear people say today: "It is impossible for things to continue as they are, with the rich getting richer and the poor getting poorer; with some gorging themselves and others starving; with injustice and misery everywhere. There must be a revolution! We are ready for it. The time is now. And this revolution is inspired by God!"

Why is it that this utterly self-evident evangelical message seems so new to so many of the faithful? How did we lose that taste for battle, and that tension toward a better future, which characterized Christianity in its original form?

The religion of the Hebrews was wholly oriented toward the future. The Bible is full of messianic hope *for this world*. It predicts, and anticipates with impatience, the revenge of the poor and the downtrodden against their oppressors. The *Magnificat* is no less revolutionary than the *Internationale*.

The first Christians awaited the second coming of Jesus in their own lifetime. Jesus would then take them with him to "the place that he has prepared" for them. And that would resolve the political, social, and economic problems from which they suffered.

But this hope, disappointed as it was doomed to be in such a naïve form, was transposed by later generations from this world into the next, into an eternity of bliss. We would join Christ individually, after our death. This evasive interpretation made earthly tasks seem useless and unimportant. And thus, generations of Christians followed one another in a world that had become nothing more than a stage in their existence, and could no longer be the object of their hope.

This loss of interest in the world, and of vitality and tension with respect to the future, left the way open to messianic political systems. Marxism, thanks to its realism and its collective dimension, won the following and excited the enthusiasm that Christianity had lost. Teilhard de Chardin said, prophetically, "The world will belong to the one who offers to it, on this earth, the greatest measure of hope." And St. Peter proudly advised his followers: "Always have your answer ready for people who ask you the reason for the hope that you all have" (I Peter 3:15).

What is this Christian hope for the world? We must avoid two extremes in trying to find out. First, we must not think that Christ has, in effect, demobilized us by making us turn away from this world in such a way that the world becomes merely a springboard for our personal salvation. And, second, we must not believe that there exists a predetermined strategy, a "divine plan" which God will realize through the Church or that he will execute by intervening in his own good time.

There is no political system based on Scripture. But there are innumerable political systems contrary to and condemned by Scripture. And there exists in Scripture a basic political inspiration: to free man from the limitations imposed on him by nature and by sin. In other words, we must work to make mankind free, loving, and responsible. We must do away with the structures of violence and injustice. And this inspiration must be implemented by means of analyses and acts that man must extemporize according to circumstances.

The basic meaning of the Resurrection of Jesus is that, henceforth, *all things are possible* to man, and that his slavery is ended since death, "his final enemy," has been overcome. There is no longer any need for human resignation. Nature and sin are no longer more powerful than

man. Man is free. Man is, so to speak, possible. Christ
has introduced unlimited hope into the world. The stone
over the entrance to the tomb has been rolled away,
broken into pieces, and man is rising to undertake the
immense task of his collective liberation.

The reason that Jesus regards as blessed the poor and
those who hunger after justice is that such men are open
to the prodigious force of liberation that calls man to
endless progress. The Kingdom of God, which is liberation, is built by human effort in order to provide a world
that is more human. It is already present in those
places where men have thrown off their chains. It belongs to those who take part in the struggle. Those who
are satisfied, the rich, are not blessed because they have
no hope.

The Church, rich, powerful, established as she is, has
a long road to travel in order to become a poor Church,
the Church of the poor. Bound to the world, for better
or for worse, she can only give life to the world if she is
able first to give life to herself. She cannot work a revolution for others unless she is capable of working one for
herself. This revolution, this transformation of the world,
is the measure and the beginning of the Kingdom of God.
And that is why it is so urgent.